An insider's exposé of British Indian Restaurant cookery

DAVE LOYDEN

with

ALAN CASTREE

Published by the Authors

Copyright © 2010

A CIP catalogue record for this book is available from the British Library.

ISBN: 978-0-9565257-0-3

Printed and bound in the UK by CPI Mackays, Chatham ME5 8TD

Front cover design and art work: Simon Harris and Tracey Purkis

(trace.simon@gmail.com)

Visit **UNDERCOVER CURRY** ™ at www.undercovercurry.com

CONTENTS

COOKING PREPARATION

MEALS

SIDE DISHES

MEALS (cont.)

SIDE DISHES (cont.)

MAIN DISHES

Chicken recipes

Beef and lamb recipes

You need to know – *this is not your usual cookbook, and so...*

you can't disregard the introductory stuff as mere chatter, as many of us often do, and flip straight to the recipes that interest you.

Not only is this a book *about* British Indian restaurant (BIR) curry as much as it is a curry cookbook, it's also a book more about techniques than ingredients. You are certainly informed of the ingredients – including those of a genuine BIR gravy – but they are only part of the story. In order to gain the results you are looking for you also need a full knowledge of the techniques to employ.

So relax, read the book and find out just what those secrets and necessary preparations and techniques are, and you'll be nicely on your way to a real BIR cooking experience, whether you're already a dab hand or a raw beginner. Anyway, you'll be on your feet and cooking soon enough, if you want – by page 8, in fact.

You'll find that the standard means of measuring used throughout the book, and that which is used by the restaurant chefs, is the curry spoon. If this is new to you, until you get your own curry spoon, use the teaspoon equivalents which are given on page 61.

If you are *determined* to jump ahead (it won't work) at least read page 63 first.

FOREWORD

Dave was only a casual acquaintance when he invited my wife and me to his place for a curry night (no surprise) with a group of his friends. These nights are a key part of Brunei's expat calendar, I later found out. We enjoyed a great night with a good bunch of friendly people, and the curry was better than I thought it could be.

During the evening I overheard Dave chatting to some of the guests. They were complimenting him on the great food and I caught snatches of his reply – "Been an obsession... devoted three years of my life... undercover work... secrets... must write a book..."

He had my attention. This sounds interesting, I thought, so I joined the group and gathered some of the details. But you know parties – it's hard to have a quiet conversation. I'd heard enough, though, to know that I wanted to know more, so Dave and I agreed to meet the next day and talk again. We did, and I was hooked.

Here's what I learned...

A party boy in his early days, Dave settled down a bit and in the late eighties/early nineties established the Dash Dispatch courier/delivery company in Aberdeen. At peak periods there were about twenty employees so it was natural that at times, when a real rush was on or someone was ill, he was short-staffed, so he would fill in. This must have happened too often because in the course of seven years Dave was hospitalized so many times that, "It would be fair to say I was a regular at Emergency". Motor bikes on wet nights can be tricky. Eventually the doctors suggested he should look for a less accident-prone occupation because they were concerned about the number of X-rays he'd had. So Dave sold up.

There was a move to Liverpool in '95 for his wife Zu to do her MD training there, and with time on his hands Dave was soon looking for pubs with unused kitchens, found them, and by arrangement with the licensee, hosted curry nights. The customers were happy, but Dave rated his culinary efforts as only 'good enough' and badly wanted to do better.

Various stints, including one on the banks of the Mersey where Dave and his cousin, billed as 'The Curry Consultants', packed in the customers, gave Dave yet more opportunity to ply his passion.

Then it was back to Aberdeen, and now the real story begins.

By this time Dave was recognised as an excellent curry cook, British Indian Restaurant style. The only one not completely happy with his skill and knowledge was Dave himself – because he knew there was still plenty hidden from him, in particular, the 'trade secrets' that were the *actual* trade secrets. He knew the only way to discover them was to be directly involved in the British Indian restaurant cooking process.

But how to get a toe in the door?

Well really, it was obvious, wasn't it? As a personable adult with an abiding passion for curry, coupled with a 'back of the hand' knowledge of the highways and byways of Aberdeen gained from seven years of delivery experience in those very streets, he was the ideal man for a delivery job. A vacancy came up and Dave was in – and all his past resolve to be done with the dangers of delivering was out the window. For a curry fanatic the prize at the end of the race was too great.

But did the change from successful businessman to deliverer of curries require a bit of an adjustment? Certainly not. It marked the beginning of the realization of a dream.

So began three years of experience in the curry trade – mainly at Aberdeen's best restaurant. It could seat one hundred; it ran three evening sittings, and you had to book.

After doing deliveries for some time and becoming an accepted part of the show, Dave started coming in early, helping out with the 'prep'. He was *in the kitchen!* Not that he was permitted to cook, of course. But in amongst peeling the onions and garlic and washing the dishes, he was listening, watching, remembering.

Perhaps the book's title is a bit misleading, though. Listening to Dave reminisce soon makes it obvious that he formed close ties with his Bangladeshi friends, and they quite openly gave their advice. "For that particular dish you need this kind of pan" and "The best filling for a Peshwari nan is..." There was a solid friendship underpinning the work relationships; they were a team. Dave might pick up their kids from school one day, and bring in some vegetables from his home garden on another. And then, of course, there was the football or cricket to discuss and dissect. If Dave was a curry fanatic, they were football and cricket fanatics.

When I heard this story I was indeed hooked. I felt that Dave's knowledge shouldn't lie idle, that a book should be written. It was clear that Dave wanted to write not just a book of curry recipes, but rather a book about curries, about the results of his search – a dedicated, unrelenting search for specific flavours and aromas. In short, a book written for curry fanatics by a curry fanatic.

Have you ever wondered, for example, as you were enjoying your restaurant meal, just what it was like 'backstage'; what was happening back there in the kitchen; what the atmosphere was like? The stories are here.

This book nicely meets the needs of those who simply enjoy an occasional curry and would really like to know how to serve up genuine BIR curry meals from their own kitchens. For those who regard curry cooking as more of an art than a craft, who know that perfection is worth striving for, who relish the opportunity to cook a dish that is uniquely their own in flavour, this book will meet their needs too, because it's written by a man with a passion for curry that borders on an obsession.

Certainly, there are a great many who dream of discovering how to reproduce those particular BIR flavours in their own kitchens. It's also true that for many of these the dream hasn't been an idle one; the desire to know has been matched with much thought and experimentation. But even amongst the most ardent enthusiasts there would be few prepared to dedicate three years of a working life to a single-minded quest of discovery. You're about to meet someone who did.

Over to you, Dave.

Alan Castree
Co-writer, editor and friend.

INTRODUCTION

British Indian Restaurants are now part of the UK psyche. They are, in the words of one recent commentator, as British as the Sunday roast and fish and chips.

However BIRs don't, in fact, serve standard Indian cuisine at all! Rather, the cuisine is the outcome of a long process of experimentation that has taken place over the past fifty years or so, beginning in Bradford and Birmingham in the early 'sixties, when Bangladeshi chefs began designing recipes that, although undoubtedly Indian, were specifically aimed at satisfying the indigenous British palate. And it is this crucial point which seems to be overlooked by most curry cookbooks.

It seems that either the authors themselves don't know the vital differences between traditional Indian and BIR cuisines, nor the particular tricks and methods of British Indian Restaurant cooking, or they do, but don't want you to know. In too many books important information is either missing, or only half the truth, or just plain wrong, and the same comment applies even to the teachings of some celebrity chefs who have ventured into the field.

This is not to criticise. There are some excellent books around giving accurate information on, and insights into, Indian cooking. It's just that – unlike this book – they don't specifically address the unique flavours and methods of traditional British Indian restaurant cuisine.

"Undercover Curry" doesn't pretend, doesn't attempt, to be a standard cookbook. There aren't pages of pretty pictures, for example. Instead, we have concentrated on making the book as functional as possible. There's a user friendly recipe layout, and when you're cooking, with the book open on your kitchen bench, you'll find that you can still easily read the instructions.

 Although recipes for all the standard dishes are given in the latter part of the book, the early sections deal with the background, the techniques and the tricks and secrets of the trade.

The fact that curry – which is not a difficult dish to make when you know how – is the best-selling carry out food in the UK clearly suggests that 'BIR how to' hasn't yet been made available to the general public, the welter of curry cookbooks notwithstanding. Our intention is that this book will correct that.

So let's dispel some myths right from the start. An Indian restaurant is like any other business – it operates to make a profit. This means that in a restaurant kitchen, time is money, and that means there just isn't the time to do the sorts of things many of the books recommend. Roasting, grinding or tapping something on your elbow four times might produce a certain flavour, but it simply won't be a BIR flavour. The fact is that most of the spices and flavourings the restaurants use are prepared commercially and are available from your local Asian grocer for pennies. The real secrets of BIR cooking lie in how the ingredients are combined and in the way they are cooked. In BIR cooking, technique is everything – and that is just what this book is about.

With the correct preparation done beforehand you can have a BIR quality meal on your table *in under fifteen minutes, night after night for weeks ahead*.

So just what are these secret preparations, combinations and techniques? You're about to find out.

FIRST DISH – *Tarka dhal*

You probably bought this book with great expectations, so before you spend time preparing and cooking the core ingredients, you should have the opportunity to get straight into a simple dish that is nonetheless one of those iconic dishes we all immediately associate with British Indian restaurant cuisine. Despite the fact that it generally doesn't contain gravy, it is nonetheless considered to have that legendary BIR flavour and it's certainly not the only dish on your Indian restaurant menu to do without gravy.

So what's this dish that lets us immediately proceed with the BIR adventure? It's the one and only tarka dhal. Grab last night's leftover chapatti from the fridge and let's substantiate the claims made on the cover of this book. With that done you can proceed with confidence.

What is a tarka?

Simply this. Once you have cooked your main meal, take another frying pan, put in a bit of oil or ghee and fry some garlic and/or some dried whole spices, allowing their flavours to infuse into the oil. Then just pour the contents of the whole pan over your main curry dish. That's it.

This method is used extensively in BIR kitchens and it's a very neat way to add your favourite flavours to your curry. Experiment widely with the tarka, using any spices that take your fancy. Who knows what flavours and aromas you may discover? And you won't be just blindly following a recipe, you'll be putting a stamp of individuality on your curries; you'll be involved in the process of creation. By making a different tarka each time, you will soon find the one that is exactly right for you, and that one is yours.

Just remember that there are few steadfast rules, and don't measure anything. (Exercise some caution, though. In BIR cookery, less is more – it's often just a pinch of this and a pinch of that. The worst thing you can do is use too much of an ingredient.) But apart from that, it's really all about you. You know the tastes and aromas you like, so use this book to help you discover the combinations and techniques that produce them. With BIR cooking it's often not *what* you cook or what ingredients you use but *how* you cook them that makes the difference.

This recipe for tarka dhal is a prime example of that. There are just a few ingredients, but by using the right cooking methods the result you get is almost miraculous. You *can* cook a masterpiece in your own kitchen. Who says that BIR curry can't be replicated at home? It can, and you're about to prove it.

Tarka dhal

You need:

> 1 small packet of **yellow lentils**, soaked for a few hours or overnight.
> **salt** to taste.
> 1 bunch of **coriander**, including stalks, chopped finely. (This recipe is a good way to use up any spare stalks.)
> vegetable **oil.**
> 1 bulb of **garlic**, cloves separated, peeled, and each sliced into 5 or 6 pieces. (Later, after we've been through the gravy process and you have some on hand you could add a little, but it's not really necessary. It's just as nice without.)

> ....

After rinsing them thoroughly, place the **lentils** into a saucepan and add just enough water to cover them. This is important as you don't want the lentils to end up all watery; you can always add more water later if you need to. Cooking them this way allows the lentils to keep more of their integrity, which adds to the quality of the dish. Now add a generous measure of **salt**. I've never measured it but I'd guess at least a teaspoon. The salt is essential to the flavour of this recipe, and it helps to soften the lentils. Once the lentils are soft, whisk them with a fork, breaking some of them down but leaving most of them whole. Then leave them to cool down and to form a thick paste.

OK, that's all the prep done. Now, take your heavy-based frying pan and add as much of the **cooled lentil paste** as needed. (For example, 3-4 tablespoons would be enough for two people.) Add **water** until you've reached your desired consistency. Some like it thick, others a bit thinner – it's up to you. Now onto the stove with it and heat it through. When you've got a nice boil going, turn the heat down to a simmer and throw in a generous handful of the **coriander**. Give it a good stir and then place it in a serving dish.

Right, that's the dhal done. Now for the tarka.

Take a small frying pan, add a tablespoon or so of **oil** and a really good handful of the **garlic**. Don't have the heat too high as the garlic will brown too quickly, but do cook it until it is brown around the outside. You may find that some of it looks slightly burned, but don't worry about that; this is the right way to cook garlic. Once it's sticky, pour the contents of the whole pan over the lentils, stir, and your tarka is ready to serve. It's that simple. Simplicity is, in fact, a BIR cooking characteristic (although there are many years of experimentation encapsulated within that simplicity).

The first time you try adding your choice of spices, record your assessment here.

NOTES – Tarka dhal

CORE PREPARATION

Probably the most important part of British Indian restaurant cooking is the preparation of the core ingredients. Every recipe contains some of them, most recipes contain many, everything depends on them, and when they are on hand you can have the finished dish on the plate in no time – as you would know from the speed at which restaurants serve your meal. Naturally, they make these core ingredients in bulk, and this is just what you should do. Put the initial effort in, divide the results into appropriate portions, freeze, and you're set for a great many top quality BIR meals that need only minimal additional work.

You'll find that I repeatedly urge you to do things your own way. Although I'll give you plenty of suggestions to experiment with I'll usually then say… "But it's up to you." However, in this case I want to push hard for a particular notion – that of doing your core preparation in bulk. It saves so much time in the long run, and it really will allow you to get a meal on the table – and one that matches that of a good restaurant – in minutes.

The core ingredients are:

- garlic and ginger puree
- tomato puree
- tandoori marinade
- the curry gravy or sauce (naturally)
- some general sauces – onion, patia, and vindaloo.

However, initial core preparation can take time, and I'd like to get you started on some genuine British Indian Restaurant cooking very early on, so we'll just do the garlic and ginger puree for now, and the gravy and the others can wait for a while. Here we go.

Garlic

Garlic is used in almost all of your favourite curries, and ginger is its frequent companion, so we'll deal with them first.

The curry houses use a large plastic container, which originally contained spices or ice cream or something similar, and fill it to the brim with garlic bulbs. Water is then poured into the container, right to the top, and then it's set aside for a few hours to let the dry garlic bulbs soak up the water. This is done last thing at night or early in the day so that the garlic is sufficiently soaked by the time it is needed. After soaking, the garlic skin peels off very easily, making a normally laborious task much less time-consuming. In my home kitchen, though, all I do is get a big tea mug, put in the separated garlic cloves, fill it up with tap water and get on with something else for a bit.

To peel the garlic, take a small, sharp knife, go to the squared off woody end of the clove and cut through so as to almost remove the woody bit but stopping just before you get to the skin. Pull the knife towards you and the skin will just come away. Then go to the pointy end and pull off any skin that remains.

Ginger

How many times have you seen celebrity chefs give you handy tips for peeling fresh ginger root? The last one I saw said to use a teaspoon! Well, actually that probably would work quite well – if you could manage to keep hold of the ginger long enough before it slips out of your hands and falls to the floor. The fact is that in all my years in a BIR kitchen I never saw anyone peel ginger – not once. I don't know if the reason for that was to do with its flavour, or if it was just another way the busy kitchen hands saved a bit of time. But as a man who wanted to cook an authentic, yummy, BIR curry at home, I decided that the safest move was to do it their way. Peeling ginger the way I used to may have contributed to me not obtaining that particular restaurant flavour, and that just wasn't an option. So now it simply gets a quick wash under the tap and then it's for the chop.

You select a method, but either way it is then chopped into manageable-sized pieces for your blender, ready to be blended into a smooth paste.

Garlic and Ginger Puree

For this you will need your soaked and peeled **garlic**, the washed and chopped **ginger**, a cup full of high quality **oil** such as canola, and a jug blender. (If you're going to make garlic chilli chicken or tarka dhal soon you might want to reserve a handful of garlic cloves, but otherwise just use the lot.)

Start with the ginger and fill the blender to about half its depth. Now, just judging by eye, add a little more than *half* as much garlic. (This is not an exact science. You'll find that you don't do much measuring when following my directions – and you'll become a better and more confident curry chef because of it.)

Now add a cupful of **oil** and blend until smooth. Add more oil if it's needed to get it really smooth.

Placed in an airtight container in the fridge, this keeps for months. After it has matured for a week or two, have a sniff. Gracing your nose will be one of those magical, mystical aromas that made you love curry in the first place.

....

We'll do the big one in the BIR curry process – making the gravy – in a moment. But there's a prerequisite, and it's one which onion bhajis can provide.

Onion bhajis

These are so easy to make when you know how, but of the many recipes I've seen for these, not one comes close to how they are actually made in BIR restaurants. So, *here's* how. (The ingredients are listed at the end of the discussion.)

I generally use 3-4 kg of **onions**, perhaps 20. This will make about 120-150 bhajis, and you can freeze them. (Even for my own family of just three I usually cook this number because it saves a lot of time in the long run – and takes only half an hour anyway.) Peel the onions, chop them in halves, then quarters. Then slice them finely lengthwise into thin strips, say 2 centimetres (about an inch) long, and 3-5 mm thick at the widest point. (If the onions were still whole you'd be slicing them end to end.)

Place the strips in a nice big bowl, take your **salt** container and shake it in a circle around the bowl two or three times. One curry spoon would be ample. (See page 61 for teaspoon equivalents and page 58 if the curry spoon is new to you.) Thoroughly mix the salt in with your hands, getting it right through the onions. When you're satisfied this has been done let them stand for an hour or two. In this time the salt will draw all the fluids out of the onions.

Then mix again. To check that you've got the salt right, dip your fingers into the juices at the bottom of the bowl and lick your fingertips. They should have a lovely oniony flavour that is just slightly salty. (If you think you need to make some adjustment to the salt quantity next time, record that in the '*NOTES*' section which follows.)

Another reason for adding the salt is that it changes the texture of the onions. If you bend one of the onion pieces before salt is added, it will snap. But after the salt has drawn out the water the onion loses this crispness, so that when you make your onion bhajis they are easily shaped into a nice round ball. Without the salt you'd have bits of onion breaking off or sticking out through the batter, so the bhajis would be hard to shape and would look odd.

Add the other ingredients – a level curry spoon of each of **curry powder, cumin, coriander and turmeric**, then a pinch of **asafoetida powder** and finally two curry spoons of the vital **ginger and garlic puree**. I also recommend that you use some

whole spices – *just a small pinch of*, say, **coriander seed** (crushed a little with a rolling pin or the back of a broad knife), **cumin seed, ajwain** and perhaps **fennel**. Again, thoroughly mix by hand. (This is important. Give up using spoons all the time. With a little experience you'll develop a much keener sense of your mixtures with your hands.)

Now add **gram flour**. How much? The BIR chefs just open the packet and sprinkle the flour over the onions so that it covers the whole surface. (If you later think you could improve the result with a little more or a little less of something, write yourself a reminder in the '*NOTES*' section on page 17. However, having said all of this, the flour to onion ratio is given in the list of 'Ingredients' which follows.) Add 2 curry spoons of either self-raising flour or bread flour and 2 dessertspoons of baking powder and stir in.

Right. Crack an **egg** or two into the bowl – two eggs for 20 onions, one for 5-10 onions - and you're about to give it a good mix. If getting your hands sticky bothers you, just dip them into a bowl of water first (but then give them a shake, as you don't want to add too much water to the mixture.) Mix thoroughly. You'll finish up with a nice gooey mass containing inch-long onion strips; all the moisture from the onions is in the bowl.

At the stove, put the **oil** into the wok – about half full. And now a strong word of caution. What you've read in other books about the temperature of your oil is probably wrong. Do NOT cook in hot oil. Heat the oil on a *low* setting. This is the way they do it in the restaurants. If you use a high temperature the mix will go dark or black because the spices will burn.

Dip your hands into a bowl of water, then pick up some of the mixture and roll it, shaping it into a ball – very satisfying. Place it into the wok so that oil bubbles slowly away around it. Repeat. Depending on their size, you can get 10-20 in a wok at a time. You'll see the colour of the oil change, you'll smell the marvellous aromas and you'll know that all the flavours are permeating both the bhajis and the oil – *the same oil which will later be used to make the gravy. This ploy is one of the keys in creating that unique BIR character,*

So… your bhajis bubble away slowly for 10-12 minutes. When the time is up and the bhajis have that beautiful, light golden colour, use a big 10 inch slotted spoon to remove them. You'll find they're soft and moist. Allow them to cool on paper towels so that the oil drains.

Later, just before you are ready to serve the bhajis, THIS is the time you use hot oil, so turn up the heat. The temperature is right when a bit of water flicked into the oil produces a sizzle. Fry them for a few minutes, depending on the temperature of the oil, by which time the surface of each will be dark brown and at restaurant crispness, leaving the inside… ahh! (Test the crispness with the edge of the curry spoon until it is as you like it.)

That's it! It's that easy, and you'll be an instant hero to family and friends alike. (And remember – retain the oil for your gravy.)

Onion bhaji ingredients

The quantities suggested will make about 120 bhajis. Whatever quantities you choose to use, the gram flour weight should always be ¼ of the onion weight.

- **onions** (4 kg)
- **salt** (as directed)
- **curry powder** (2 curry spoons)
- **garlic and ginger puree** (2 curry spoons)
- **coriander seed** (small pinch)
- **cumin seed** (small pinch)
- **ajwain** (small pinch)
- **flour, gram** (1 kg)

- **bread or S.R. flour** (2 curry spoons)
- **baking powder** (2 dessertspoons)
- **eggs** (2)
- **oil**

The critical ingredient in onion bhajis is salt.

....

Salt is essential both for flavour and for softening the onion, allowing the bhajis to be properly shaped

---

NOTES – Onion bhajis

Cook onion bhajis on a low heat until the final few minutes.

This stops the spices from burning and keeps the bhajis moist inside, while the hotter oil at the end gives them their crisp coating.

The good oil

Have you ever wondered, as you sat in a restaurant after eating your favourite curry, savouring the taste of all those subtle flavours on your tongue, just how the chefs manage to combine such a wide variety of spices – garlic, ginger, cumin, coriander, fennel, ajwain – and yet still keep the overall flavour so subtle? Well, you've already taken the first step towards discovering the answer.

If you want your curries to have that real BIR taste, then sometime before making the gravy you should make some fried snacks and starters, save the oil and use it in the gravy. This oil – from the onion bhajis, samosas, pakoras or whatever – is subtly infused with all the spices used in their making. When these are incorporated into your gravy, your home cooked curry will be just like those from your favourite curry house.

This was the method used in all the places I worked in.

Save cooking oil used in making starters for when you make your next gravy.

THE GRAVY

Right, now to the big one. First, just what is the BIR gravy? What's its story?

Well, before the advent of British Indian restaurants the migrant workers from India and Pakistan (and mainly Bangladesh in the early days) needed to cook for themselves. They found UK food either too expensive or unpalatable – or both. They seriously missed the spicy foods of their homelands.

Then some of the entrepreneurial among them began to realize that there was a gap in the food market in Britain – an opening for a new, tastier and spicy style of cooking, yet not authentic Indian food. The need was for Indian food with a British slant, and so back in the 'sixties a quiet food revolution began. In the process of devising really tasty meals that were both quite cheap and quick to prepare, the one pot style of cookery was devised – a technique quite similar to the stock pot of European cookery.

A ladle or two from the one large pot on the back of the stove (the gravy) would go into almost every dish that was created by these chefs. Then just by either changing the garnish, or by the addition (or omission) of one or two ingredients, a vast range of curries, of many varied flavours and aromas, could be quickly produced, and because the core ingredients of the gravy were indigenous to the UK they were also very cheap to prepare. (In one conversation, a restaurateur told me that a gravy that cost him £25 to produce would later make curries to the value of £2500 in the restaurant.)

So the gravy is really the essence of it all. It is critical, certainly, but at the same time it is flexible. During the final fry, for one dish the chef might add a bit of mango chutney and to the next, a dash of lime pickle, and hey presto, you have two completely different flavoured sauces, which in turn generate different flavoured curries.

The production of this all important gravy can differ from restaurant to restaurant, but only very slightly. It is widely considered amongst them that a good gravy will have the same 18 base ingredients, with one or two possible additions at the chef's discretion. Some chefs like to add a bit of jaggery (unrefined palm sugar) to it while others like a mild aniseed overtone. Again, such choices are up to you. Initially, make the gravy exactly as detailed below, but on later occasions by all means experiment.

And this leads me to an important point. One characteristic that will assist you in your BIR cooking is boldness. Don't worry about making mistakes, because some of your greatest successes in your BIR adventure can result from what you thought were mistakes; they will sometimes turn out to be great discoveries.

This has certainly happened to me. We had guests for dinner and, of course, curry was on the menu. I was faffing around rushing here and there doing the curry chef routine and nearly ready to serve when suddenly a friend said, "Oh, it's lamb is it? I don't really eat red meat. Could I possibly have a vegetarian dish instead?"

I bravely said, "Of course!" but thought to myself, "Hmm…" and, with fingers crossed, went looking in the fridge. Thankfully there was some okra and some parboiled spuds, and I rushed over to the stove to make a hurried bindi aloo. But in my haste I somehow forgot to add the garlic and ginger puree AND the tandoori masala and it wasn't till I placed the dish on the table that I realized what I'd done. I hesitated, then had a quick taste and… I was mesmerized! Gracing my taste buds was one of those magnificent, sought after flavours that had eluded me for years.

Now remember, this wasn't due to something I'd added. It was due to something I'd left out, and that's worth keeping in mind when you feel in the mood for a little experimentation.

It's true that I learned the most while undercover but I did, and still do, come across a few good ideas in my own kitchen.

Right, enough. Let's get to it…

MAKING THE GRAVY

At some stage you've got to decide how much gravy you want to make – just enough for a meal or two, perhaps? Or do you fancy making a good deal more and freezing it? I very strongly recommend the latter. It makes sense to me. To make enough for many meals takes only a little more time and effort than is needed to make enough for just a single meal.

I use the same pan for gravy whether I'm cooking for a restaurant, a large group of friends or just my family. This way, in one go I get about forty portions of gravy, which lasts our family for a long time, even though we have curry most evenings.

For weeks ahead I can have a top class Indian restaurant meal on the table in ten minutes, sometimes less – and so can you.

So I'll start with the bulk method and then give you the amounts for a small quantity if you're really determined to do it that way.

Making a large quantity

(Before we start, note that all the vegetables are only rough chopped because they're all going into the blender.)

Right, here we go. I use a big pan – a big stock pot – which holds 16 quarts, that is, about 18 litres. Scale the ingredient quantities down if you use a somewhat smaller pot.

Get a big bag of **onions** and peel enough to fill approximately ¾ of the pan. Then in goes a small **cabbage**, 4 medium-sized **carrots**, 1 **red pepper** and 1 **green pepper**,

4 curry spoons of **garlic and ginger puree** (that's about 16 dessertspoons), two tins of **tomatoes** or a couple of big curry spoons of **tomato paste**, and then your spices.

Spices

I use 2 curry spoons of each of **salt, coriander, cumin, asafoetida (hing), ground fenugreek seed**, and **curry powder**, but a little less of **turmeric**, say 1-2 curry spoons. (A little chilli powder is an option.) Second last in is the **coriander**, with the stalks chopped into 2 cm lengths (so that they don't jam the blender later – the stalks can be tough). By now the pot will be piled up, but not to worry.

Now add **oil**. You need at least a litre of the oil that you've cooked your snacks in – the onion bhajis, or vegetable pakoras, samosas… If there's not a litre, use what you have and top it up with some unused vegetable oil. (I like to use a non-GM canola oil. It's high in Omega-3 fatty acids, and low in Omega-6 acids. Sunflower oil and many others are high in Omega-6.) Finally, add 1½ to 2 cups of **water**.

There are 18 ingredients in a typical BIR gravy. Check them off.

The secrets are out, and a BIR gravy is within your grasp.

Now for a bit of patience. Plonk the pot on the stove on a very low heat, the lowest you can get, with the lid on if it will fit. It will warm very gradually, and as it cooks the moisture will come out of the ingredients. You started with the pan almost brimming over but the vegetables gradually reduce, releasing their moisture and flavours into the oil. (This is a BIR secret that restaurant owners would prefer you didn't know about.) Because of the reduction the lid will soon go on.

One reason for the low heat is that as the cooking proceeds and the moisture reduces into the oil, the spices sink to the bottom, and with normal heat they inevitably burn onto the bottom of the pan. But if you are cooking on the lowest heat possible, the resulting degree of burning won't have a detrimental effect on the end result.

Don't stir at all until the moisture comes out of the vegetables, raising the fluid level significantly. Then stir from time to time, but don't scrape the bottom of the pan. Leave any residue just sitting there. (When you do stir, lean over and inhale – one of those mystical BIR aromas will be wafting about. How many times has it lured you into a restaurant, powerless to resist? Well, this time it will be coming from your own kitchen.)

After the vegetables have reduced sufficiently (after about 40-60 minutes, and with the level now about two inches below the top), you will see a film of oil covering them. This means you're getting close. Take the pan off the stove and let it cool with the lid on – don't transfer it to another container until it is cool. Then it's over to the blender.

You are now about to begin transferring the gravy from the pot to the blender in stages, only just half filling it on each occasion. Each time, initially pulse the contents a few times before changing to full power, and patiently wait until the puree is REALLY, REALLY smooth. (Don't use one of those food processer type blenders that have the blade that goes right across the bottom of the base. It won't puree the gravy thoroughly enough and the resulting mix will have a kind of grainy texture – and that isn't good enough.) Repeat this blending process until all the gravy has been pureed. If you are using a hand blender and blending inside the pan itself, once again persevere until you have converted the mix to a totally smooth, grain free puree.

Once the gravy is smoothly ground you should have a yellow mixture that is a bit darker than turmeric. What you've got now is an emulsion of the vegetable oil, the pureed vegetables – with all of their tasty juices – and water. (When back on the stove the heat will separate the oil from the rest and undo that emulsion, but more about that shortly.)

You are now ready for the final cooking stage. After washing the pot to remove any residue on the base, *half-fill* it with the pureed mixture and then *add water* to return the level to about two inches from the top (low enough to prevent boiling over). This is a critical step. You are diluting the gravy with an almost equal amount of water.

(If you have a little taste you won't yet recognize any BIR flavours, but all the same, whatever you do, don't think 'Oh, it needs a bit of this or it needs a bit of that.' That is the very worst thing you could do at this stage. Go in trust.)

Thoroughly stir the pot's contents then heat it to a roiling simmer. It will froth after it has simmered for some time, and you will need to take the lid off. This froth is what some publications describe as a scum appearing on the gravy surface, and some advise that you skim this off. DO NOT DO THIS. This 'scum' is oil bubbles that will form a layer of oil on top of your gravy and *which is essential to obtaining that BIR curry flavour.* (It is the separation of the oil from the emulsion, referred to above, and will dissipate after a further 10-15 minutes of simmering.)

About 40 minutes or more after you began the final cooking stage you will see the oil separating from the gravy. Take the pan off the stove, replace the lid and leave it. After a minute or so, go back to the pan and check. If the entire surface is covered with red oil then it's ready. If you don't have that result, it's back to the stove for a while. (You may need to add a little water to replace any lost through evaporation.) Keep repeating the test until the entire surface of the gravy is covered in a layer of red oil. When it is, the gravy is done.

Remember that although the whole exercise might take some time, it's easy enough, *and you're laying the critical foundation for everything that lies ahead.* With the right gravy, the world's your oyster – and those BIR tastes are quite achievable.

One 16 litre stock pot will fill 17 of the 1 litre SKP containers (allowing for expansion during freezing) that you'll have from takeaway meals, and as you have doubled the mix by diluting it with an equal amount of water, you get sufficient gravy for about 34 meals for a family of three from a single gravy cook-up. You freeze it – it keeps for months. Now that's worth thinking about! If you have, say, three curry meals a week at your house, there's about a 2½ month supply of BIR quality gravy there in your freezer.

You can take a container from the freezer the night before. Or, for immediate use, run some cold water over the base and drop the contents into a second pan and heat through until it is boiling. (It is best if the gravy is piping hot before it is added to the final fry.)

Making a small quantity of gravy

Remember, all vegetables are rough chopped, as they are going to be blended.
Using a small saucepan of say 2 litres, you will need…

- onions, enough to about ¾ fill the pan
- carrot ,1 medium-sized
- cabbage, 1 handful
- red and green capsicum, ½ small of each
- garlic and ginger puree, 1 dessertspoon
- ½ tin tomatoes with fluid
- Spices: 1 dessertspoon each of salt, coriander, cumin, asafoetida (hing), ground fenugreek seed, curry powder, turmeric
- coriander, with the stalks chopped into one inch lengths

- about 200 ml of oil (preferably saved from earlier cooking, as described previously)
- ¾ cup of water

The method is as before. Again, don't worry if initially you can't get the lid on. As the cooking proceeds the vegetable mass will reduce, the fluid level will rise to cover the vegetables and the lid will fit.

When cooking your gravy, DON'T skim off the top froth.

It's an essential part of the gravy.

Gravy summary

(The detail given above is necessary to ensure that you get this critical element of BIR cookery just right, but detail can make a process appear far more complex than it really is. This summary should help to put the process in perspective.)

<u>Ingredients</u> There are 18:- onions, cabbage, carrots, red pepper, green pepper, garlic & ginger puree, tomatoes (or paste), salt, coriander, cumin, asafoetida, ground fenugreek seed, curry powder, turmeric, coriander, oil, water.

<u>Method</u> Vegetables in pot; oil (1-1½ litres for the large pot); 1½ cups water; cook on lowest heat; lid on as best as it will fit (it will fit as the vegetable mass falls); oil film on surface after about 40-60 minutes; remove pot from stove and allow to cool (lid on); transfer to blender in stages, half filling it each time, blend until *totally* smooth; mix the puree thoroughly and return enough to the pot to half fill it, then raise the level with water to nearly full; stir; heat with lid off, simmering until the oil

separates from the gravy (again, about 40-60 minutes); take off stove. In a minute or so a red oil should cover the entire surface. If it does, the gravy is done. If not, return the pot to heat, then re-test.

Use the above procedure for the remaining half.

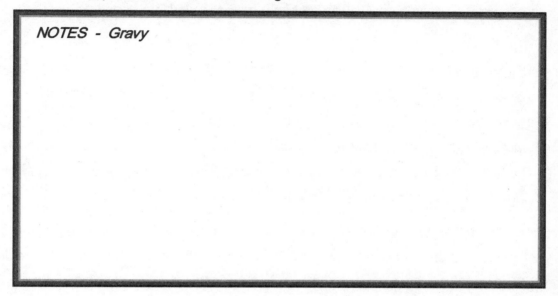

NOTES - Gravy

Comments and gripes

I've already said that cooking your own BIR curry is not an *exact* science, but there is a lot of science involved – in fact, probably more science than cookery. But in contrast with most cookbooks, in this book you will only rarely see exact quantities given as they were in the gravy recipes. Exact measures are appropriate for cakes, but for Indian cooking? – hardly. As soon as you develop confidence I very strongly recommend that you don't measure anything. (Unless it's with your big curry spoon – which I assure you will become a great friend of yours in achieving your ambition to emulate those great British Indian restaurant curries.)

Another of my big arguments with cookbooks is the use of the teaspoon as the world's defining measurement for all recipes. You won't find a set of scales in an Indian restaurant kitchen – or a chef running around with a teaspoon. The chefs there don't slavishly follow a recipe. They need the freedom to create, and cooking for them is a passion – a skill, an art and a craft all rolled into one. If you want to replicate the meals they produce in curry houses then do it their way.

The big problem with the 'a teaspoon of this and a teaspoon of that' approach is that you're going to end up with about 20 grams of spices in a meal for two, and that's way too much. With this book I hope to break you free from the mould of any teaspoon mentality. So take up your curry spoon, and make your dream a reality. The skill of spice addition requires a touch and finesse that is simply not possible when you're using teaspoons as the unit of measurement.

And this points to yet another advantage of cooking a large quantity of gravy at a time. Curries are certainly tasty, but they're very subtly spiced, and cooking in bulk gives you much finer control over the amount of each ingredient. You will have much more success (and much less work overall) if you cook a large quantity of gravy each time.

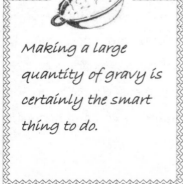

Making a large quantity of gravy is certainly the smart thing to do.

There are many advantages:

- *you save so much time in the long run*
- *and anyway, it doesn't take much more time than it does to make enough for just one meal*
- *it freezes well and you have enough for meals for weeks and weeks ahead*

Tandoori marinade

This is another *key element* in BIR cooking. Although famously known for its role in chicken tikka, tandoori marinade is used extensively. It's another way of combining ingredients, another way of placing that third layer of flavours.

The first step in this process is to make your own yoghurt. It costs too much to buy, and the process is child's play. You can mix the starter yoghurt with as much milk as you like, but I usually pour 2 litres of **full cream milk** into a pan (to get a nice, creamy yoghurt).

Bring this to the boil and boil for a couple of minutes. Take it off the stove and allow it to cool, with the lid on, until it's at body temperature – when it feels neither hot nor cold to your finger. At this stage a little tub of **natural yoghurt** is added. Give it a whisk and leave it in a warm place overnight with the lid on. The next morning you'll have 2½ litres of yoghurt.

Now for the marinade. First, ¾ fill your jug blender with your home-made **yoghurt** and add one dessertspoon of each of these three pastes – **tandoori, tikka** and **curry paste** (Kashmiri is a popular paste choice in the restaurants.) If you have only one of these pastes, that will do, but use just 1½ -2 dessertspoons of it.

Now form your hand into a little cup, shake in some **cumin powder** and throw it in the blender. Then do the same with **coriander, turmeric** and **curry powder**. Add a dessertspoon of **mint sauce**, the juice of a **lemon** (or a lime, or both, or the zest of a lemon), some **cumin seeds** (just a pinch), a pinch of **fennel**, some **ajwain** (ground carom seeds) and some **red food colouring** (although that's up to you, you're in charge. I add it because I want it to look like a restaurant dish as well as taste like one, but…) Then on with the blender and zap it. Don't worry if you find there's food colouring sticking to the sides of the jug. You can turn the blender off after a minute, give everything a good stir with your curry spoon, and zap it again for a bit longer.

You now have one of those top Indian restaurant flavours lurking in there. Bottle it, and you can use it for your dips, poppadums, onion bhajis, dips for snacks or as a marinade for tandoori beef, chicken, prawns… Whatever. It's good to have a stock of this beside your cooker so that you can put it into your curry *because it has the most dramatic effect* – greater than almost anything else you might do to your curry. The effect is mind boggling. A splash of this will completely transform a curry that is just ordinary – the colour, the flavour, the aroma. The curry comes alive, and you'll be thinking to yourself 'Ah ha, I'm a chef!'

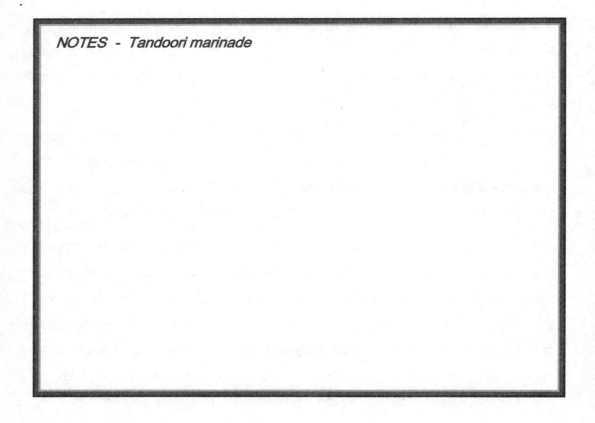

NOTES - *Tandoori marinade*

Tomato puree

Sometimes at a restaurant with an open kitchen you might be invited to go in and watch the chef at work and see for yourself what he's doing. That experience can help you learn the secrets of some dishes, but not tomato puree. All you'll see is a red, pureed paste, but in some curry houses there is much more than just tomato puree hidden away inside.

I found this out before I started working at Indian restaurants. At the time I was getting my meals from a 'starter' restaurant (premises rented out to an aspiring chef who hopes to make a name for himself after a time, develop a clientele and then move on to setting up his own restaurant). Now this particular Bangladeshi chef was a master chef in the making and when I watched him making my usual order of chicken vindaloo and a garlic nan, I noticed that the colour of the tomato puree wasn't quite as usual, so I asked, "Is that just tomato puree?"

"Yes, that's all," came the answer.

"Do you mind if I have a little taste of it?"

He didn't, and put some in a little container and brought it over to the counter. I dipped a finger in, tasted it, and it was obvious it wasn't just tomato puree. So I said, "That's not just tomato puree. What else have you got in there?"

He just laughed and replied, "Well, I'm not going to tell you. You'll just have to guess."

One of his chefs called out, "I don't think you'll get it."

Now there's a challenge!

So I smelled it, tasted it again, and rolled it around the tongue, and I knew that I knew it, but... and suddenly there it was.

"Tandoori masala!" I cried out to the circle of chefs that had gathered.

They all applauded happily and were then quite ready to open up. The puree contained tomato puree, tandoori masala, a bit of garlic powder, a little vegetable oil and the mix was watered down slightly.

So you never know where you're going to pick up that extra bit of information that makes a difference. I couldn't wait to get home and make my own. Later on in the restaurants, I learned that most use a slight variation of the above.

To make tomato puree

You have two choices – use ready made or make your own. To make my own I start with a tube of **double concentrated tomato paste** from the supermarket. (Most restaurants seem to use the same Greek paste for some reason. It's called 'Star', and comes in a big container.) This concentrate goes into a 750 ml microwavable plastic container you get from the take-away. (I also use these containers for storing spices.) Add a bit of vegetable **oil** and then some **water** until, after stirring, the mix is the consistency of thick custard. Add a level teaspoon of **tandoori masala** and a level teaspoon of **ginger powder**, and stir in well. That's the tomato puree done. It's fine if it has a slight purple tinge. If it is quite purple, though, you've used too much tandoori masala.

Here's an alternative you could consider. If you also add a little garlic powder to the tomato puree, you can often omit the tandoori masala step when doing the 'dipping', using this form of tomato puree as its replacement. This is a more subtle way of including tandoori masala flavours, well suited to those who don't like things too spicy, and it is probably a more authentic way of doing things. Over time, try both and see which is best for you.

In either case, wash out a left over takeaway container, pour in your tomato puree and place the container beside your cooker, along with all your other spices.

Apart from the sauces, this wraps up the key elements of the core preparation. (By the way, when a restaurant tells you that their dishes are made with their own special blend of spices, perhaps roasted and ground, take the information with 'a large pinch of salt', because in my experience it's rarely true. The chefs are just too busy to prepare their own blends. There is, though, a special curry powder that restaurants use, but you can only buy it in catering quantities. It comes in a 10 kg drum, and is made by 'Rajah'. It's called 'Premium Madras Curry Powder', but you can't get it in a small pack. However, at your Indian grocer you'll get either the 'Rajah Hot Madras Curry Powder' or the 'Mild Madras' and these are good alternatives.)

Dave's Tip

Lime or mixed pickle is also a nice addition to the tomato puree.

NOTES – Tomato puree

"Tomato puree" is more than just tomato puree.

The restaurants make their own using

- tomato paste
- oil
- water
- tandoori masala
- ginger powder

Arranged around your cooker

Remember that before you start cooking a particular dish, any dish, you will surround yourself with the majority of these base ingredients.

- gravy
- garlic and ginger puree
- tomato puree
- tandoori masala
- herbs and spices
- salt
- curry powder
- ground cumin
- (garam masala)
- chilli powder
- lime or mixed pickle (bought), preferably pureed in a blender before use
- tandoori marinade

With these, and armed with your curry spoon and heavy-based frying pan, you're ready to make the curry of your choice.

Later on in the book I'll give you the recipes. I'll stick mainly to the old favourites, because old style traditional is the focus of this book, and also because most of the other recipes are just minor variations of the old favourites anyway.

You can add all, or any, or as few of the above core ingredients to any curry. If you're making a dish for the first time, it's better to stick to the recipe given, but after that a recipe is merely a set of suggestions, not rules. There are no rules – apart from those you make for yourself. Whatever you do is going to be good, very good. Just remember – when you *do* get a result that to your taste is just *perfect*, make a note of what you did. You've just invented your own signature dish.

Garam masala

This is the one exception to the comment made earlier that restaurants generally don't make their own spice mixtures, but merely buy them off the shelf.

Why the exception? Because garam masala is simple to make, quick to prepare, and uses common spices. You take equal amounts of **cloves**, **black cardamom**, **black peppercorns** and **cinnamon** and grind the mixture in a coffee grinder until it is really fine. Alternatively, you can buy already ground spices in small packets from your Asian grocer. Get a packet of each spice, mix them together, and it's done.

Most restaurants I've had experience with use garam masala in the preparation of their curries and it's only from personal taste that I prefer to use tandoori masala instead. Tandoori masala contains approximately twenty spices compared to the four to six commonly used in garam masala, so it brings many additional and subtle flavours to a curry, including amchoor (mango powder), celery powder, nutmeg, lemon powder and star anise.

If you do like to use garam masala, my advice would be to refrain from using it at the dipping stage (discussed later), when the spices are normally added. Rather, use tandoori masala but have the garam masala ready in a large pepper shaker. As soon as the curry you've made is poured into the serving dish, take this pepper pot and give it two brisk shakes over the prepared dish.

This is a method commonly used in the BIR kitchen, with the only difference being that they use an old food colouring container with a single hole about the diameter of a pencil with the instructions from the boss, "Two shakes, do not squeeze" and they then stir it in with the serving spoon. In some kitchens they also employ this method to add dried mixed herbs, thyme powder and powdered methi leaves to a dish.

The problem with adding garam masala at the dipping stage is that the flavours are too intense. You want the flavours to merely make a guest appearance on the tongue, to be hinted at, rather than having the whole dish infused with them.

NOTES – Garam masala

CORE PREPARATION

SAUCES

Onion sauce

This sauce is an essential addition to a dopiazza, but it can also be added in small amounts to any dish, imparting a silky, mildly sweetly-spiced, BIR loveliness.

To prepare the **onions**, peel them, cut them in half, then cut each half down the middle. Slice thinly from end to end and you're left with little strips an inch or so long. Almost fill a medium-sized saucepan with the sliced onions, then top it to the brim with sliced **green capsicum**. Add one or two little ears of **star anise** and just one **clove.**

Now pour in enough **gravy** to half fill the pan. Cover it with a very tightly fitting lid and cook on the lowest heat possible for a few hours, stirring occasionally.

The restaurant where I learned to make this sauce would cook it for at least 8 hours. So you can cook it for as long as you like, providing the heat is as low as you can get it and the lid is very tight to prevent any reduction – you need to retain these flavoursome fluids. If you have one, a slow cooker is very suitable for this dish.

Vindaloo sauce

It's true that in most areas of life you can't please everybody, but with curries you usually can. Some like a hot curry and others like it very hot; some like it a bit spicy while others like it mild.

Now, if you add a little vindaloo sauce to a mildly spiced curry it peps it right up. So with just a flick of your curry spoon you can cater to all tastes. Make a bhuna, say, nice and mild to suit your boss's wife and serve her, then stir a little vindaloo sauce into the remaining curry and as if by magic you're presenting your boss with a lovely hot chicken bhuna vindaloo seconds later.

So how do you make vindaloo sauce? You need **dried red chillies** (with their seeds), **white vinegar, lime or lemon juice, cumin powder, coriander powder, salt, oil, tomato puree, gravy**, and for the fire-eaters only, hot chilli powder.

Use enough **dried red chillies** (stalks removed, seeds left in) to ¾ fill an average jug blender. Add 2 or 3 glugs of white vinegar (**apple cider vinegar** works really well) and 2 really good squirts of **lemon or lime juice** (I prefer lime). Throw in a bit of **cumin powder** from the bowl of your hand and then the same of **coriander powder** and **salt**. Next add a glug or two of **oil**, ½ a tube of **tomato puree**, enough **gravy** to cover the jug's contents, and... some extra hot chilli powder if you so desire.

Zap it all in the blender until it is totally smooth with no traces of chilli left. Transfer it to the frying pan and cook on a low to medium heat until the oil separates and the sauce is thick. The thicker it is, the hotter it will be. You decide how hot you want it to be.

(This is a concentrated sauce, but you may have some guests who want their curry made using this as the gravy! So be it. It's each to their own, and proof that there really is a curry for everyone.)

Patia sauce

This is the final sauce in the group of additions that you'll often have laid out around the stove before you begin cooking specific dishes. You need:

- equal amounts of **mango chutney, tomato sauce, pineapple juice** – say a cupful of each.
- about a quarter to a half of this (¼ -½ cupful) of **mint sauce**. This provides the sour element of your sauce, so adjust the amount of mint to suit your taste.

Place all in the blender, blend, then add **red food colouring**. And that's it. Easy!

If you can avoid it, don't use cold gravy when making a curry.

It's best that gravy is piping hot when it's added to the final fry.

PRE-COOKED MEATS (See page 63 for suggested recipe quantities.)

All the meat used in a restaurant BIR curry is pre-cooked. This enables the chef to get curries from order to table in the minimum amount of time, and so keep the customers happy.

When you are thinking about pre-cooking meats, here's something to consider. You know that a casserole always tastes better the day after it's cooked, as the flavours have had time to permeate the dish. Well, the same argument applies even to pre-cooked meats, so I suggest that you cook them a day or two before they are needed. (Cook double amounts to save work later, if you wish.) After cold storage you'll find they develop a delectable flavour which greatly enhances any curry dish. The restaurants cook all the meats in a gravy and water mix. On completion this liquid can be reserved, refrigerated, and used as gravy when cooking the actual dishes.

Chicken (BONELESS BREAST)

You can pre-cook the chicken breast in a variety of ways; your choice will largely depend on how much time you have. The easiest and quickest way is to lob one straight out of the bag and into a steamer for 15 minutes. There's no need to even handle the raw chicken. Cut it into pieces after it is cooked, or alternatively, when making your curry simply throw the breast into the pan whole and break it up with your curry spoon.

The way it's done in most restaurants

Take the whole, uncooked chicken breast, turn it on its back and remove that long thin flap. In it you'll find a white length of sinew. Remove this. (Curry houses steam and use the flaps for chicken pakoras, but you can put them in any curry.)

Now cut across the end of each breast to get two bite-sized chunks. Then slice the breast first down the centre and then across until you have formed 6 or 8 similar sized chunks. Place the cut **chicken** into the saucepan and half cover it with **gravy**. Then add enough **water** to just cover it. Heat to a simmer and cook for 5-10 minutes.

As usual, there are options open to you. Some restaurants like to sprinkle in some mustard or agwain seed, cumin or a little ear of aniseed as the chicken is cooking; others cook the chicken very vigorously until the gravy and water evaporate, leaving a very mildly spiced chicken base with which to start a curry. Once again, it's your call. Experiment and discover.

Beef

Its treatment is similar to that of chicken. Cut the **meat** into bite-sized chunks, place them in a pan, add **gravy** to about halfway up the meat, add a glug of **oil** and then enough **water** to just cover. Then, as beef has a stronger flavour than chicken, in order to get that BIR flavour you really do need to add some subtle flavourings to complement it, as follows.

In a dry pan roast a few pinches of **methi seed**, **cumin seed** and **ajwain** until they become fragrant, and tip them into the main pan.

Then add:

- a generous pinch of **methi leaf**
- a couple of **black** and **green cardamom pods**
- a few good pinches of **nutmeg**
- a few **bay leaves**
- a pinch of **hing** and a pinch of **ground methi seed**

and season with a generous pinch of **salt**. Add a good splash of **vegetable oil** or ghee. Heat, then simmer until the water evaporates, leaving the meat with a thick, glossy coating of gravy and oil. Test the meat by squeezing it between your fingers. If it's tender, it's done. If not, add a little more water and cook until tender.

Once done, leave to cool and the contents will thicken up nicely. You should be able to make out the chunks of meat inside this very thick savoury coating.

Lamb

Lamb is similar to beef but has an even stronger flavour, so cook it the same way with the same ingredients, then add a small handful of **flaked almonds** and a splash of **pineapple juice** followed by a squeeze of either **lemon or lime juice**.

………………………………………………………..

These few tips are my own variations, but I believe that they add much to the dishes, and those I've cooked for have recognised this. The procedures transform a standard dish into something vastly more impressive.

Chicken tikka.

Use pre-cooked chicken (see page 40). Add enough **tandoori marinade** to just cover each piece of chicken, then place the bowl in the fridge for half an hour, or even overnight. This will thicken the marinade so that it sticks nicely to the meat; the colder the meat the more the yoghurt component of the marinade sticks to it.

Get some bamboo skewers and put 5-6 pieces of meat on each, making sure none of the pieces are touching. Place the skewers on a roasting dish or similar, again making sure that no meat is touching. (There are small aluminium foil trays that are slightly longer than the skewers and support them at either end.) Pop the tray into the oven on high. They are done if, when you squeeze the chicken between your fingers, it wants to break up, and the ends of each piece are beginning to blacken. If it's rubbery, it's not done.

Repeat the process till all are cooked.

Beef, lamb, fish and prawn tikka are cooked in precisely the same way as chicken tikka. You even pre-cook them in the same way that chicken is pre-cooked.

Cook meats beforehand – enough for more than one meal.

Following each of the above quick and simple methods gives a special result, and cooking enough for later meals gives you that 'on the table in 10 minutes' bonus.

RICE

What gets my goat more than anything else about some curry houses is the way they skimp on the rice. After all, rice is still relatively cheap (and that's true for even the finest, most expensive, aged Pakistani basmati rice), especially when you consider that just one cupful is more than enough for one person.

Storing and buying rice

When I lived in the UK I used to buy the very best Pakistani basmati rice in a 45 kilo sack and this would last my wife, our son and me for ten months. I urge you to do the same.

Why? The longer rice is stored the more it matures and the more intense its flavour and aroma become. You can ignore the 'use by' date if you store it correctly, and that's easy enough – simply put it in a large, airtight, food grade container. I always leave the same tea cup inside the container, and use one cup per person.

Cooking rice

- If you can, always use the same pan.
- If you cook conventionally, never fill the pan more than ⅓ full of rice. With American long grain, the rice to water ratio is about 1:2. For Basmati rice, the rice to water ratio is about 1:1½. Basmati also takes less time to cook. Start with the rice in cold water, bring it to the boil, then cook it for about 10 minutes.
- Alternatively, consider my own method which follows. By using it you'll get the grain integrity the best restaurants do, and as a bonus you'll never overcook the rice, which is easy to do if you just boil it.

Palau Rice

Here are some tips on how to cook a Palau rice that would be worthy of the most illustrious curry house. It's a two stage cooking process – the rice is first lightly fried in oil, then later boiled in water.

<u>Here's what you *don't* do</u>. I'll bet you've been told that the first thing to do with rice is to give it a good rinse. Well, not this rice. Basmati is the king of them all and washing it will leave each grain with less integrity. As a result, the grains of the finished dish won't stand to attention in the pan, as they should.

<u>Here's what you do</u>. Place the desired quantity of the best Basmati you can get your hands on into a *bone dry* pan and add a small quantity of cooking **oil**. Place the pan on a fairly high heat, and as the rice heats, stir to prevent it from sticking. There should be just enough oil to coat each grain of rice. If there is any extra in the base of the pan, pour it out. As you continue to stir you will notice the rice starts to turn from opaque to white. If some grains do stick to the pan, they may turn a light brown, but don't worry about that. The brown grains give a lovely nutty flavour to the rice. In fact, it's nice to have a scattering of brown speckles through the rice, adding both flavour and colour. However, you need to scrape them off the bottom of the pan before they turn black.

Once you're satisfied that most of the rice has changed colour, take the pan off the stove and pour in enough **milk** to make it bubble up. Then rest it. It's important to do this before you add any flavourings, otherwise these will be too intense. (You can, however, use thin coconut milk instead of normal milk if you wish.) Then add your flavourings – yes, *before* adding the water for boiling. You could try **cloves, green cardamom, bay leaves, cassia bark** and **star anise**. **Ground almonds** or **cashews** are good and **grated lemon** or **lime peel** is nice too. Try one or two of these.

Now add the **water** (for every measure of rice add 1½ measures of water) and cover the pan with a very tight fitting lid. Place it on a high heat until steam starts to escape. *As soon as this happens, remove it from the heat.*

All your rice needs now is enough heat to keep it warm for ten minutes. You can achieve this in a number of ways. At home I have a hob with four gas rings and two electric plates and for warming I use the smallest electric plate on its lowest setting. Alternatively, if you have a bain marie use that, or else place the rice pan over a larger pan of boiling water and just let it steam gently away. Even the heat of a candle is sufficient. Another way is to just turn off the ring you were using, leaving the pan to quietly steam as the ring cools.

After ten minutes all the water will be absorbed and you should notice the grains on the top standing as if to attention. Your rice is now cooked and is ready to be used immediately, straight out of the pan. However, you may want to colour it.

How to colour your rice

I know that getting that BIR taste is your main goal, but the appearance of your curry is also important. If your rice looks good you anticipate a wonderful flavour before you taste even a single morsel. Your guests will be impressed with your ability to present them with a curry that not only smells and tastes as good as, or even better than, one from their favourite curry house, but also *looks* like a curry house rice. Serving at home or for guests, the aim is for the total effect, and appearance, aroma and taste each has its role to play. Colouring the rice will not alter its flavour in any way, but it will give it that more authentic BIR look.

The colouring is added as soon as you take the rice off the stove. I use a liquid colouring consisting of equal amounts of yellow, green and red. It's essential that you don't use too much and the best way to ensure that is to use just half a capful of each. When you take off the pan lid, mentally visualize a cross in the pan separating the rice into four sections and, in turn, scatter just one colour into each of three of the four sections, leaving one section with no colouring. Place the lid back on the pan and leave it for ten minutes. Then empty the rice into a container large enough to allow you to give the rice a good stir to mix all the colours evenly throughout. Replace the lid slightly offset, so that the steam can escape.

Now that you've finished the cooking process, stir the rice to incorporate some air, so that when it cools you'll have separate grains instead of lumps.

When the rice cools, observe that each grain is completely separate. Bite a grain and you'll find it has an appealing al dente quality. This is the result of frying the rice at the start of cooking and it's this al dente integrity that will enable you to work with the rice further without it going mushy. For example, you may want to make a biryani. This will involve using some gravy, and with this rice you will get away with it. But if you added gravy to plain boiled rice, you may well end up with a plate of mush.

Finally, whether you use this method or the conventional one, it's important to remember that rice should be cold before you add it to a dish. I like to cook my Basmati rice the day before I use it.

(The same applies to noodles. If you add hot, just cooked noodles to a dish you're likely to end up with a gluggy mess.)

NOTES – Palau rice

Want to cook rice perfectly? There is more to it than just boiling it – but it's worth the extra effort!

- buy the best Basmati
- store long-term in an airtight container
- don't rinse it
- first cook in oil, then add milk, then rest it
- add flavourings <u>before</u> the water
- use less water than for other rice
- remove pot from heat as soon as it steams
- let stand 10 minutes then colour
- stir to incorporate air; use cold if adding to a dish

BREADS

Battora

This bread is my favourite. It's a little unusual as it uses yoghurt instead of oil, but it's similar to chapattis in that you don't need to measure anything. You just guess the quantities you need, mix, and then simply add either extra flour or yoghurt as needed to obtain the desired consistency, which in this case is a fairly dry dough. It should be sticky enough to hold a shape when you are kneading, but dry enough that none of the dough sticks to your fingers as you knead.

When you roll the dough, remember that it will puff up as it fries, so allow for this thickening. Roll out to about normal pastry thickness.

....

Ingredients

- flour, plain white
- salt, pinch
- yoghurt
- oil for frying

....

1. Put the flour into a bowl, keeping it less than half full. (1 kg of flour will make about 12-15 battoras. Adjust quantities to fit your needs.)
2. Add a pinch of salt.
3. Pour in the *blended* yoghurt (see Dave's Tips) and mix it in very well.
4. Knead these ingredients and adjust the mix with extra flour or yoghurt until the dough will hold a shape but doesn't stick to the hands. Form it into small balls.
5. Lightly flour the rolling pin and surface and roll each ball into a saucer-sized circle of about normal pastry thickness.

6. Heat the oil in a pan, and fry the battoras on each side for about 10 seconds plus, depending on the oil's temperature. Remove them when they have puffed up, but before they go brown. Cover.

Dave's Tips

Most books suggest that you add the yoghurt to the flour just as it is, but *don't do this.* The majority of chefs first pour the yoghurt into the blender (perhaps with a little lime or lemon juice), and then blitz it. This will change its consistency from its usual thickness into something much thinner.

NOTES - Battora

Chapattis

Chapattis are a much loved, quintessentially Indian food. They're iconic, they're delicious, and they're just *so* easy to make. (Although there is a secret to it.)

Firstly, ignore recipes that give you exact amounts of this or that ingredient. Forget that – nothing is measured. You'll see chapattis being made by street vendors in almost every village in India, and often in S.E. Asia. No one measures anything, and this is one of the reasons they're so easy to make – all you need is a bowl and a pan.

And why is nothing measured? Because as with battoras, relative quantities are determined by the consistency of the dough. It has to be sticky enough to hold a shape but dry enough so that when you're kneading it, none sticks to your fingers – that is, a fairly dry dough. So if it does stick, add a little flour, but if it's too dry and it crumbles, add some water.

Chapatti flour is called atta, and it's freely available at any Asian grocer and some supermarkets. However, I believe that if you make up your own mix of:

    3 parts white bread flour
    1 part wholemeal bread flour

it actually gives a better result. Try it sometime.

If this is your first time making chapattis, as a guide to quantities, a cereal bowl of flour will make four to five.

Here we go.

....

- flour (atta or alternative)
- salt
- oil
- water

....

1. Half fill your mixing bowl with flour.

2. Add a sprinkle of salt.

3. Pour in a glug of vegetable oil.

4. Add a little water.

5. Mix together with a fork initially, and then with your fingers. Adjust the consistency by adding small amounts of flour or water (not oil).

6. When the consistency is right, wrap the dough in cling film and put it in the fridge for at least 20 minutes.

7. Then take it out of the fridge and form the dough into balls which, when rolled out, form circles 15-20 cm (6-8 inches) in diameter. (These can be quite thin because they will thicken in the pan.)

8. Use a well-seasoned dry pan or steel tava. Place a dough circle onto the heated surface. Cook until little black spots begin to form, then flip and similarly cook the other side. Use tongs to lift it out and it's done. (But you can then hold it over a gas flame to blacken it a little more – which is what many chefs and street vendors do.)

9. Repeat until all are done.

> *Dave's Tips*
>
> Many books give you exact amounts of ingredients and tell you that the result will be perfect chapattis. But after you've followed the instructions, disappointment awaits because the result is usually far from perfect. Take good note of steps 6 and 7 above. It's necessary to rest the dough, and it's best to cover each circle with cling film after it's rolled out, unless it's going straight into the pan. *Then* you'll get perfect chapattis. (And they are dead easy, aren't they?)

Nan breads

You can make a variety of nans, such as garlic and keema (spiced mince meat), but *Peshwari* nan is the one we'll do.

First we have to make the nan dough. It's easy and fast, but there's a lot of waiting time in between, so you may as well make sufficient for a good number of nans, as some can be kept in the fridge to be re-warmed at a later date. This recipe will make about 12-15 nans. (Here's another of those rare occasions in which more precise ingredient quantities are required.)

Nan dough

....

- flour (1 kg, plain or bread)
- salt (1 dessertspoon)
- baking powder (1 dessertspoon)
- milk (500 ml)
- yeast (1 sachet)
- sugar (caster, 3 dessertspoons)
- eggs (2)

....

1. Put the flour into a bowl. You may need a little for adjusting the dough consistency if you don't get it just right the first time, so reserve a little.
2. Add the dessertspoons of salt and baking powder.
3. Pour the milk into a jug and bring it up to body temperature by adding a little boiling water. (Reserve just a little for possible dough consistency adjustments.) Add the sachet of yeast and the 3 dessertspoons of caster sugar to the milk jug and stir well to dissolve them.
4. Make a well in the centre of the flour; pour in the milk, yeast and sugar mix.
5. Add the 2 eggs.
6. Mix as well as you can with a spoon, then get your hands into the dough

and give it a good knead. It should hold together well but not stick to the bowl. (If you grab a handful of dough at the top and twist, the whole clump should turn in the bowl.) Adjust as needed with small additions of milk or flour.

7. Lift the whole ball of dough out of the bowl, then slam it back hard, then do it again – give it a couple of really good thumps.

8. Put the bowl aside in a warm place, cover with cling film, and leave it until you can *see* that it is bigger. This might take about 20 minutes. (If you are using a small bowl and the dough might touch the cling film as it rises, lightly oil the film.)

That's the nan dough done. Now to convert this to bread.

Nans

9. Separate the dough into balls – about 12 or a few more – so that they each will roll out into circles about 15 cm in diameter.

10. Place these on a baking tray, cover with lightly oiled cling film and leave in a warm place to double in size. This will take about 2 hours.

11. Rub a little vegetable oil onto your hands and roll a nan ball between them to incorporate the oil. Place it on a lightly oiled surface and roll it out into a circle.

12. Add a touch more oil to your hands and rub them lightly over the nan surface. Then lift the nan and place it on the extended fingers and thumb of your upturned other hand, held in front of you. With your now free hand, grab the dough near the upturned thumb and in a single motion pull it towards you and down, into a tear shape. (You don't have to do this, but it's how the restaurants give their nans that typical tear shape.)

13. Place it onto a lightly oiled baking tray, and repeat 11 and 12 till the tray is full.

14. Put the tray into an oven, pre-heated on highest setting. Cook for about 8-10 minutes or until the nans are golden brown and their surfaces are lightly bubbled. (If you like them crispy, cook a little longer.)

(This mix will give you nice, chewy nans. If you prefer them fluffy, use a milk and yoghurt mix instead of the milk alone.)

Peshwari nan

A Peshwari nan is a nan with a rather delicious filling, and the recipe below makes a heap of it. Make the filling while your nan dough is rising (see step 10 on the previous page).

....

- fruit cocktail (tin)
- almonds or cashews (ground, small packet)
- sugar (level curry spoon)
- desiccated coconut
- sultanas (two good handfuls)
- melted ghee (for brushing)

....

1. Pre-heat oven, highest setting.
2. Empty the contents (fruit and juice) of the tin of **fruit cocktail** into a jug blender.
3. Add the ground **nuts** and the **sugar**, and then blitz the mix until it's a very smooth puree.
4. With the blender still on, and its lid on, remove the lid plug and through the hole slowly add the **desiccated coconut** (see Dave's Tips) until the contents form a thick paste (like play dough).
5. Transfer the mix to a bowl, throw in the **sultanas**, and knead. The consistency should allow you to do this.
6. Take a lump of the risen nan dough, make it into a ball, then plug your thumb into its centre, forming the dough into a cup shape. Take a suitable amount of the Peshwari filling, pack it into this cup, then squeeze the open edges of the dough together to form a complete seal. Roll the resulting ball between your hands again, place it on a very lightly oiled surface and roll out to thin. Place it on a heated tray and pop it into the pre-heated oven.

7. When it looks done – puffed up and with a bit of brown – then out it comes to be brushed with melted **ghee**.

Dave's Tips

You can roast the coconut beforehand if you like – or even just half of it. They wouldn't bother doing this in the restaurants, but it does add a nice additional flavour.

NOTES – Peshwari nan

Bread variations

Garlic nan is made by simply brushing a puree of garlic butter over the rolled out nan before cooking.

Keema nan is made the same way as Peshwari nan, but with a filling of cooked, spicy, mince meat.

COOKING PREPARATION

Pots, pans and utensils

Preparing BIR food is easier if you have the following items:

1 stockpot, 15 litre	As discussed in 'Making the Gravy'. It's a worthwhile purchase.
1 heavy-based cast iron frying pan	Most of your cooking will be done in this. (All the BIR chefs I've seen have used aluminium pans but I like to avoid aluminium utensils.)
1 wok	For deep frying and making biryani or Palau rice.
1 jug blender	This should not be a blender with flat, horizontal blades. The blades of a jug blender are alternately bent up or down, and this improves its effectiveness. Also, make sure that the base of the section that lifts off the motor is hard plastic (the bushes of the stepped rubber bush type wear out too quickly).
1 large mixing bowl *(preferably china)*	For doughs, onion bhajis.
1 large stainless steel curry spoon	This is an essential. It's like a large tablespoon but with a long handle – its total length is about 30 cm. It's used to 'dip' (see page 58).
1 saucepan	Primarily for cooking rice.

1 rolling pin	For chapattis and other breads.
1 small knife	For preparing garlic.
1 larger knife	For chopping onions.
1 roasting tin	For chicken tikka, kebabs.
1 pkt. of bamboo skewers	There are about 200 of them per packet and so they'll last you for ages.
plastic containers	Those used by the take-away restaurants are fine. Use them to store the spices, chopped/sliced onions and peppers, garlic and ginger puree, vegetable oil, chutney and pickles, curry powder, salt, tandoori masala, chopped coriander, gravy, etc. Use either a container or a bottle for tandoori marinade. Have them gathered around you when you're cooking.
2 large airtight containers	One for storing the various spice packets (both ground and whole) and one for your rice.
1 slotted spoon	For taking onion bhajis and vegetable pakoras out of the wok.
1 ladle	Needed from time to time, e.g. for transferring gravy to the blender.

Dipping – *the technique*

Dipping is an essential skill, but a simple one. Hold your curry spoon as it is shown in the diagram below – approximately horizontal, edge down. Hold it above the container, tilt it slightly back from the vertical, and point the tip slightly down. Then just dab its edge into your container of spice, puree or marinade. Tap the contents of each dip into the pan and repeat the procedure for each spice in turn.

It doesn't matter if your initial attempts don't result in the suggested amounts shown in the diagram below; if you take too much or too little you just empty the spoon back into the container and try again. And take your time – you don't need to be as fast as the restaurant chefs. You'll find that in no time you'll be dipping with ease and a style all of your own.

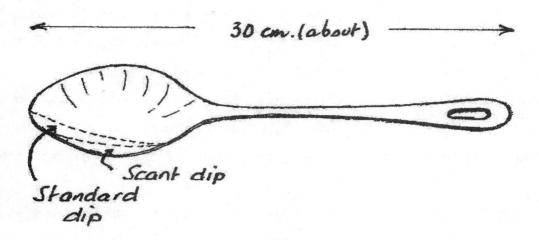

Test your skill: ten standard dips into your spice container should result in about seven teaspoons of spice.

Reminders

You'll recall that in earlier pages, the simplicity and speed of preparing BIR meals in your own home was discussed, and you're about to experience this for yourself.

Once you've done the core preparation – made the gravy, the purees, tandoori marinade and the like – *the rest is easy and fast.* Easy, because the recipes usually follow the same basic steps and in a short time these will become second nature to you; fast, because you have already prepared most of the ingredients.

So once again, you are urged to make these core preparations in bulk and freeze them in small containers that hold sufficient for individual meals for your family. If you had to make a small quantity of each one before you began to cook the meal, it would be rather daunting. If, though, they are already prepared, and all you have to do is take the stored servings out of the freezer beforehand, then it's true – you will have the family meal, of a standard that matches that of the top restaurants, on the table in 10-15 minutes. Not only that, but you'll be able to do this for the next couple of months. It's almost dinner on demand – your meal will certainly be on the table in less time than if you ordered take away.

You are about to cook quality, BIR curries in your own home. If this is your first attempt, and you skipped some of the previous pages because you were keen to get started, at least make sure that you are familiar with the sections on core preparations and 'dipping'.

Before you start cooking

Now that you are about to begin cooking the standard dishes, it's timely to review some procedures and approaches.

1. Before you actually start cooking you will normally surround yourself with containers of these core ingredients:

    - gravy
    - garlic and ginger puree
    - tomato puree
    - tandoori masala
    - herbs and spices
    - salt
    - ground cumin
    - (garam masala)
    - chilli powder
    - tandoori marinade
    - lime or mixed pickle
    - any sauces that may be appropriate

2. The recipes which follow are mainly the old favourites, because most of the other recipes are just minor variations of them. Besides, the selection suits the nature of the book – old style, traditional British Indian restaurant cooking.

3. Remember that the recipes should be followed slavishly for the first time only and after that you should feel free to experiment.

4. Experimentation can include considering what could be omitted as well as what could be added.

5. When you are adding, do so with a light hand. It would be a shame if a potentially excellent addition was marred by excess. The old saying that 'you can add more later but you can't take anything out' is a sound one.

6. Use the 'Notes' to record your ideas of what to try next time, and the

successes (and failures) of what you did try. Your signature dishes come from those experimentations that *you* judge have produced a 'just right' result.

7. Throughout the book you've heard me railing about teaspoons and other 'exact' measures. They never use them in BIR kitchens and, for me, that fact alone is sufficient cause to be done with them.

   However, the overriding reason for not using exact measures is that I want you to develop a feel for your cooking, treating it as an acquired art rather than as a chemistry experiment. Those many among you who have already acquired that art will know just what I mean.

   While the volume of your 'one curry spoon' dip will vary a little each time you do it, this is a plus, not a negative, as the small variation will create only subtle changes, and this will allow you to find the tastes that are just right for you.

8. Point 7 notwithstanding, until you have bought your very own curry spoon, the approximate curry spoon/teaspoon equivalents are…

---

1 curry spoon *standard dip* = ¾ of a teaspoon

1 *level* curry spoon (just scraped level, not tamped) = 4 teaspoons

1 curry spoon *scoop* = 10 teaspoons

9.	You should glance again at *Dipping*, page 58.

 In the recipe section which follows, this curry spoon icon always accompanies the operation, and usually no instructions will be given. In these cases a ***standard*** dip is always implied. On the occasions when a *scant dip* is required it will be specifically stated.

(Note that when you're cooking, following the dipping stage, you'll find that much of the oil you began with has been absorbed by the spices. You need an adequate amount of oil to prevent the spices from sticking to the bottom of the pan, so simply add more oil as it is needed. Any excess can be skimmed off with the curry spoon before you proceed to the next step.)

....

Finally, remember that only the techniques are fixed. The ingredients – and the amounts of each – are variable, and in fact usually do vary from chef to chef. As this time *you* are chef, you are now most cordially invited to take over, to be in charge and cook without feeling in any way constrained by the printed word.

The Recipes – general information

Number of serves   Unless otherwise stated, all recipes provide 3-4 serves.

Preparation time   Assuming the 'core preparation' items are on hand and meats are pre-cooked, preparation and cooking time (apart from the breads) is generally about 10 minutes.

Quantities
(pre-cooked weights; 3-4 serves)

- Chicken   – 500g
- Beef/lamb – 700-800g
- Prawns   – 500g
- Vegetables – 500g

> **Precise quantities of general ingredients are not always given, but don't let that bother you.**
> **If a listing is merely 'garlic', think *'some* garlic' and add the amount that seems appropriate. Note the amount you used and after eating, record your assessment in the *'NOTES'.***

Pre-cooked meats are assumed throughout.

Ingredients (interpreting the brackets; dipping)

Any *lone* ingredient listed in brackets usually implies that it is *optional.* However a '(gravy)' entry means that you may need to add gravy to prevent the mixture from sticking as you cook. Immediately following an ingredient *quantities* are sometimes listed in brackets. For clarity, the 'dipping' ingredients are always listed separately.

Finally...

- Remember to re-read the section on cooking meats (pages 39-42). Using those methods gives the meats distinctive flavours and these contribute to the overall BIR taste of the dishes.
- Haven't bought your curry spoon yet? Check teaspoon equivalents, page 61 again, but do try to get your curry spoon at the first opportunity. It is *the* most important utensil. After all, you are about to cook like a curry chef, so you really need to be equipped like one.

All done? Excellent. Let's cook!

SIDE DISHES

BOMBAY ALOO *(Bombay potatoes)*

This is a hot, somewhat sweet dish – not overly, though. Some extra oil might be needed in the cooking.

....

- oil
- garlic
- *dipping*
- patia sauce
  (or mango chutney)
- potatoes (1-2 medium,
  pre-cooked)
- methi
- gravy

Dipping

salt

cumin

garlic & ginger puree

tandoori masala

chilli powder

....

1. Into the pan with 2 curry spoons of nicely spiced onion bhaji (or similar) **oil.**
2. Add **garlic**, and stir.
3. *Dipping* – **salt, cumin, garlic and ginger puree, tandoori masala, chilli powder.** Stir.
4. Add either **patia sauce** or **mango chutney**. (This adds sweetness, but in a natural way, without being too obvious about it.) Stir.
5. Now the **potatoes** – 1 or 2 medium, pre-cooked potatoes, chopped into bite-sized chunks. (A nice alternative is to use tinned, cold, new potatoes. This does change the flavour a little, but try it sometime.)
6. Add a good four finger pinch of **methi** (fenugreek leaf), and stir.
7. Add **gravy**, but just enough to cover. Stir.

8. Turn up the heat and reduce until it's quite thick.
   Done.

Dave's Tip

It's nice to add fresh green chillies at step 3 or 4.

NOTES – Bombay aloo

ALL RECIPES

<u>Meat quantities</u> (pre-cooked weight)
Beef & lamb: 700-800 g
Chicken & prawns: 500 g

<u>Number of serves</u>
All recipes serve 3-4

<u>Preparation time</u>
10-15 minutes

<u>Exact amount of ingredients
not stated</u>? – this point is
discussed in "General
information" on page 63.

CAULIFLOWER BHAJI

This is a lightly spiced dish – mild and slightly sweet – with a little coriander to finish.

....

- oil
- *dipping*
- mango chutney
- cauliflower (2 handfuls)
- gravy
- coriander

Dipping

garlic & ginger puree

salt

curry powder

cumin

....

1. Frying pan, **oil**.
2. *Dipping* – **garlic and ginger puree**, **salt**, **curry powder**, **cumin**.
3. Put the end of a fork into the **mango chutney** jar and add some. (If a lump goes in, chop it against the side of the pan with the curry spoon.)
4. In with the **cauliflower** – 2 handfuls of florets. Turn up the heat and give it a good stir before it starts to stick.
5. Continue stirring as you add enough **gravy** to cover, and turn up the heat.
6. Reduce until it's reached the consistency you like.
7. Finish with a pinch of fresh, chopped **coriander** leaf.

Dave's Tips

1. When dipping you may like to add some chilli powder.

2. Variations:

For aloo ghobi:- throw in some pre-cooked, diced potatoes and a bit of extra gravy and there you are. Or substitute the mango chutney for mixed vegetable or lime pickle and then you have an achari ghobi, either as a side dish or a main.

(All of which begins to explain how you can have so many dishes on a restaurant menu. So many of them vary only in a couple, or just one, ingredient.)

NOTES – Cauliflower bhaji

DIP

This is by far the most popular dip, and although the restaurants originally intended it to be used with chicken pakora, it now comes with most dishes – and is expected! "Where's my dip?" is a cry that's been heard more than once by delivery staff and more than one delivered order has been sent back by a disgruntled diner simply because no dip was included.

It comes in a variety of colours because food colouring really is needed in this dish – without it, it is an unappealing grey. Cooks variously add red, yellow or green food colouring to suit their mood or the dish it is being served with. I always use red colouring to produce a light pink dip. Whatever colour you choose, go easy with it – unless you like electric yellow dip, of course.

You may need to adjust the quantities below as this recipe provides half a jug full.

....

- tandoori marinade (½ a jug blender)
- red and green peppers (capsicum, ½ of each)
- mint sauce (1 dessertspoon)
- mango chutney (1 dessertspoon)
- roasted cumin seeds, finely ground (1-2 dessertspoons)
- coriander (handful)
- food colouring

....

If you don't have roasted cumin seeds:

Start with a dry frying pan, heat it, and throw in a handful of cumin seeds. Move them about until the aroma wafts up and the seeds begin to blacken and pop. Take them out of the pan, put them into your spice or coffee blender, and grind and grind and grind them until they are absolutely fine – like talcum powder. This is essential because you want the flavour of the roasted cumin but you don't want gritty bits of seeds.

Back to the dip:

1. Half fill a jug blender with **tandoori marinade**.

2. Add the de-seeded, broken up flesh of half of a **green** and half of a **red pepper**.

3. Add a good dessertspoon of **mint sauce**, and another of **mango chutney**.

4. Add 1-2 dessertspoons of finely ground **roasted cumin seeds**.

5. Zap it all in the blender, then add a good handful of **coriander** and blend again.

6. Add **food colouring** of your choice to convert the grey colour to something more appetising.

   It's done, and ready for your onion bhajis or vegetable pakoras, kebabs, nan bread…

Dave's Tip

If it's taking too long to grind the roasted cumin seeds finely enough, put the grinder's contents through a very fine sieve, return what's left in the sieve to the grinder, and continue grinding. Repeat if necessary until any grittiness has gone.

NOTES - Dip

KEBABS

There are two popular kebabs, and they differ only in the way the meat is formed and cooked. With a sheekh kebab the meat is skewered then grilled or oven cooked, while a shami kebab is shaped into a burger and cooked on a hot plate. In some restaurants it is placed on the top of the tandoor oven or occasionally fried by the frying chef. At home it is generally cooked on a dry or very lightly greased frying pan.

Sheekh kebab

The main thing to avoid is using too much tandoori masala. It has a yoghurt base, which tenderises meat, so too much masala makes the meat fall apart and it can't be formed into a kebab.

The meat used is either lamb or beef (I prefer lamb) but both need a certain amount of fat in them.

....

- ½ kg minced lamb (or beef)
- tandoori masala
- cumin, ground
- coriander, ground
- curry powder
- garlic & ginger puree
- *dipping*

  Optional – choose from
  - mint sauce
  - fresh coriander
  - dried fenugreek leaf

Dipping

tandoori marinade

salt

chilli powder

....

1. Place the **meat** into a mixing bowl.

2. Using a curry spoon in a similar method to dipping *but heavier*, add ⅓ of a curry spoon of each of **tandoori masala, ground cumin, ground coriander, curry powder** and **ginger and garlic puree** to the pan.

3. *Dipping* – using only the edge of the curry spoon, add just a *scant* dip of **tandoori marinade**, then a *standard* dip of **salt** and **chilli powder.**

4. Now the optionals, if you wish. My preference is for a bit of mint sauce into the lamb mix, but for you…?

5. Now comes the mixing, and it's got to be thorough. Get your hands right in there and mix and mix.

6. Time for the skewers. Take a skewer in one hand and dip it into the mix. Form an open fist with your other hand and squeeze the meat onto the skewer with a pulsating action, up and down, up and down the skewer until it is coated. Leave an inch space at either end so that the skewer can rest on the tray. Repeat.

7. Rest the skewers crosswise on a suitable baking dish or aluminium foil tray, then it's into a very hot, pre-heated oven. Every few minutes I rotate the tray 45^0 to overcome any oven hotspots.

8. Test for readiness by placing a clean dishcloth over a skewer end to hold it, and trying to tear off a piece of meat. If it breaks off easily, it's done.

Dave's Tip

I appreciate that some people choose never to use food colouring. In principle I support this attitude, but I don't mind using cochineal occasionally because it's a natural product, and I do like dishes to look tempting to the eye as well as pleasing to the palate. A bit of cochineal in the mix certainly improves the look of the kebabs (although you couldn't say the same for the look of your hands afterwards!).

MIXED VEGETABLE CURRY

For this dish restaurants usually just use the packets of frozen mixed vegetables that you can buy at any supermarket. However, a good restaurant would also add some fresh diced potatoes, some cauliflower or broccoli and sometimes either broad or butter beans, sometimes courgettes. I happen to particularly like cauliflower and butter beans as additions – yum. Again, though, the choice is yours. You might like to mentally change the name of the dish to 'Just Slightly Mixed Vegetable Curry' and use say only two or three of your favourite vegetables, or separately do, say, one lot of potatoes and one of cauliflower, and serve them in two separate bowls.

....

- oil
- ginger and garlic puree
- tomato puree
- *dipping*
- ground methi leaf
- frozen vegetables (1 pkt., plus your choice of fresh additions)
- gravy
- coriander

Dipping

salt

chilli powder

curry powder

cumin

....

1. Put 2 curry spoons of **oil** into the pan.
2. Add **garlic and ginger puree**.
3. When this starts spitting, add **tomato puree**. Stir.
4. *Dipping* – salt, chilli powder, curry powder, cumin.
5. Add a pinch of **ground methi leaf** and give the pan a good shake

and stir.

6. In with the bite-sized **vegetables** – a cereal bowl about ¾ full.

7. Add **gravy** to cover.

8. Increase heat to reduce down to dry.

9. Now a good pinch of fresh, chopped **coriander** leaf, and a final stir – done.

Dave's Tips

While you're at it, cook more than you need and use the excess as fillings for vegetable samosas or wraps. With a little imagination you can make a range of tasty snacks from leftovers. (And the same comment applies to many of the other dishes.)

NOTES – Mixed vegetable curry

SAG ALOO

This translates as spinach and potato. It's one of the most popular dishes on the menu, and is very tasty.

(I don't know of a single restaurant that bothers with the washing and chopping of fresh spinach. It's a 'time is money' issue, so they use tinned instead. However, if you're not hard pressed for time and the shops are selling lovely fresh spinach – well, fresh is best.)

....

- oil
- garlic (sliced, small handful)
- *dipping*
- (gravy)
- spinach
- potatoes (1-2 medium, pre-cooked)
- gravy
- coriander

Dipping

garlic & ginger puree

tandoori masala

salt

cumin

curry powder

....

1. **Oil** (1-2 curry spoons), in the pan, medium heat.
2. Throw in the sliced **garlic** and stir. Keep stirring. When the edges just start to go brown, in with the spices…
3. *Dipping* – **garlic & ginger puree, tandoori masala, salt, cumin** and *just a touch of* **curry powder**.

   Give the pan a good shake and stir – get the tip of the spoon right into the base of the pan. If it wants to stick or burn, add ⅓ ladle of gravy.
4. Throw in a good handful of **spinach**…

5. … and then 6-8 bite-sized chunks of the **cooked potatoes**.

6. Add 1-2 ladles of **gravy** and boil it down, stirring with the tip of the spoon.

7. Add a good pinch of fresh, chopped **coriander**, and give it a final stir.
    Done.

NOTES - Sag aloo

MAIN DISHES

CHICKEN RECIPES

Chicken achar pall

This dish is really tasty, but it's not for the fainthearted because it's hot – very hot.

…………………………………………………………………..

- oil
- *dipping*
- tomato puree
- lime or mixed vegetable pickle
- chilli flakes (dried)
- (gravy)
- red and/or green pepper (handful)
- chicken
- gravy
- coriander

Dipping

garlic & ginger puree

tandoori masala

curry powder

salt

chilli powder

cumin

…………………………………………………………….

1. Put 2 curry spoons of **oil** into a pan and heat.
2. *Dipping* – **garlic and ginger puree, tandoori masala, curry powder, salt, chilli powder, cumin.**

   (Check the 'Dipping' notes, page 58, if needed.)
3. Add ½ a curry spoon of **tomato puree.**
4. In with the **lime** or **mixed vegetable pickle**, about a forkful, and stir. If you see any big lumps of pickle, cut them up with the edge of the spoon against the side of the pan. (Give the pan a good bang with the spoon – it all adds to the effect.) Any small lumps can be left.

5. Add a level curry spoon of **dried chilli flakes**. Give it a stir. Turn the heat up slightly, but don't let it burn. If it starts to burn or stick, add ¼ of a level curry spoon of gravy and keep stirring, keep stirring.

6. Toss in a handful of sliced **red** and/or **green pepper.**

7. Add the **chicken** and stir to thoroughly coat it with the pan's contents.

8. Add **gravy**, just enough to cover the meat.

9. Give it a really good stir, reduce to the desired consistency, then add a large pinch of fresh, chopped **coriander**, and give it a good final stir. It's done.

Dave's Tips

1. You might wish to add more oil if you find that the spices have absorbed most of it. You need to have enough oil to fry them in, and it can always be skimmed off at the end.

2. You can add fresh chillies if you like, and for those that like it really hot, grind some very small, dried, red chillies – with their seeds – to a fine powder. When you add these, even the most ardent fire-eater will be satisfied.

NOTES – Chicken achar pall

Chicken bhuna

This dish has a thick sauce which is usually nice and red (although it can be a little bit brown).

I like to add tandoori marinade to this one (and a little lemon, but be careful!).

....

- oil
- tomato puree
- *dipping*
- lemon juice
- (tandoori marinade)
- chicken
- gravy
- coriander

Dipping

garlic & ginger puree

tandoori masala

curry powder

chilli powder

salt

....

1. Curry spoon, fill it with **oil,** into the pan, low heat.
2. Add 1 level curry spoon of **tomato puree,** stir, and turn the heat up slightly to get a nice, steady, but *not* vigorous bubble.
3. *Dipping* – **garlic and ginger puree**, **tandoori masala, curry powder,**
   chilli powder, salt.

   Stir away and let the aromas waft up.
4. Add a wee sprinkle of **lemon juice** (just a tiny squeeze).
5. A good option is adding ½ a level curry spoon of **tandoori marinade**. Give the pan a good stir.
6. In with the **chicken**; get each piece well coated with the sauce.
7. Add enough **gravy** to just cover the chicken. Turn the heat up a bit and keep it going until the gravy has been reduced to a really thick sauce and the chicken has a thick, sticky coating.

8. Thirty seconds before you're ready to serve, throw in a good pinch of fresh, chopped **coriander** and stir.

Dave's Tips

As well as adding to the flavour, the tandoori marinade gives the meat an attractive pink colour.

NOTES – Chicken bhuna

Chicken danzak

This is one of my real favourites (just beaten by lamb danzak). When served with vegetables, rice, and garlic nan you have a fully balanced meal: lentils and meat for protein; rice and bread for carbohydrates; vegetables (also in the gravy); and vitamins and nutrients in the spices and the pineapple.

I always have it vindaloo hot. Ahh – unbeatable!

Before making the dish, cook two heaped curry spoons of lentils, and let them cool. (If you'll be making this again in the near future, cook more and refrigerate the excess.)

....

- oil
- tomato puree
- *dipping*
- chilli powder
- (gravy)
- chicken
- lentils (pre-cooked, cold, 2 heaped curry spoons)
- gravy
- pineapple juice
- pineapple pieces (2 rings)
- coriander

Dipping

garlic and ginger puree

salt

curry powder

tandoori masala

....

1. Pan on stove, low heat. Put 1 full curry spoon of **oil** into the pan.
2. Add ½ a curry spoon of **tomato puree**.
3. *Dipping* – **garlic and ginger puree, salt, curry powder, tandoori masala.**
4. Now the **chilli powder.** (How much is up to you – you're the cook. I like it hot.)

Give it all a good stir. Turn the heat up a bit, keep stirring. If it starts to burn, add a ¼ ladle of gravy and stir it in.

5. In with the **chicken.** Make sure each piece gets a good coating.

6. Add 2 big heaped curry spoons of the **pre-cooked cold lentils.** Mix in, and mix again.

7. In with the **gravy**, just enough to cover, or even a bit less.

8. Add **pineapple juice** (2 curry spoons) and a couple of **pineapple rings**. They can be chopped or left whole to make it easier for those who really don't like pineapple. Turn the heat down.

9. When it's heated through, dip forefinger and thumb into the chopped **coriander,** and sprinkle it in. Give it a quick stir and it's done.

Dave's Tips

This one is notorious for burning. At step 6 you've got to watch for that. Stir constantly, turn the heat down and just gently heat it through.

NOTES – Chicken danzak

Chicken dopiazza

We're getting into the milder recipes now. This dish is a good one for the whole family, young or old. If you are cooking for children as well as adults, omit the optional chilli powder at the dipping stage. You can always add some after they have been served.

....

- oil
- tomato puree (¼ curry spoon)
- *dipping*
- chicken
- onion sauce (1½ curry spoons)
- gravy
- coriander

Dipping

garlic and ginger puree

curry powder

salt

tandoori masala

(chilli powder)

....

1. Frying pan on stove, low flame. Put 1 curry spoon of **oil** into the pan and give it a bit of a stir.
2. Add **tomato puree** (only ¼ of a curry spoon), and stir.
3. *Dipping* – **garlic and ginger puree, curry powder, salt, tandoori masala, chilli powder** (optional). Stir thoroughly.
4. Throw in the **chicken**, and get each piece coated.
5. Now add the **onion sauce** (1½ curry spoons) and stir it in well.
   Turn the heat up and then give it a good vigorous fry. Tip the pan to flambé it; impress your guests – bang and rattle the pan a bit (yes, just like in a curry house), and keep shaking, shaking.

6. In with the **gravy**, but just enough to cover the meat. Remember, you've already added onion sauce, and that contains gravy as well. Keep it on a high heat, and when you've got your desired consistency, add a sprinkle of fresh coriander, mix, and it's done.

Dave's Tips

1. If you've been working your way through the recipes, you'll know all about dipping. If not, the details are on page 58. But briefly, hold your curry spoon edge down and dip the edge lightly into each spice container in turn, tapping the contents into the pan each time.

2. Storing your spices in 750 ml plastic containers, such as those you buy your take-away in, allows for easy dipping. Forget teaspoons; this method is easier, faster, better.

NOTES – Chicken dopiazza

Chicken jalfrezi

This is a very versatile dish which can be transformed into many other dishes by the addition of a variety of other ingredients, each imparting its own flavour. For example, convert it to chicken jalfrezi madras by adding half a curry spoon of tomato puree with the garlic and ginger puree, and a very thin slice of lemon or lime when you add the gravy. Alternatively, make a chicken jalfrezi vindaloo merely by adding a curry spoon of vindaloo sauce. Or, a chicken jalfrezi achari bhoona with the addition of half a forkful of lime pickle and cooked until the gravy has reduced to a very thick consistency.

Thus you can, if you wish, easily make four different dishes to please four different diners at the one meal. *This is a key feature of the one pot cookery system.*

- oil
- tomato puree
- *dipping*
- (gravy)
- red & green peppers
- chillies
- mango chutney
- chicken
- gravy
- coriander

Dipping

tandoori masala

chilli powder

salt

garlic & ginger puree

curry powder

tandoori marinade

1. Put 1 curry spoon of **oil** into the pan and warm it.
2. Add **tomato puree** and stir.
3. *Dipping* – tandoori masala, chilli powder, salt, garlic and ginger puree, curry powder, tandoori marinade. Stir.

4. Keep stirring. You need to avoid any sticking here. If it wants to brown, add ¼ ladle of gravy.

5. Add a scant handful of each of **red and green pepper**, cut into strips.

6. Add whole **chillies**, and STIR.

7. Take up a little **mango chutney** on a fork, add, and stir again.
Watch out – the chutney will burn if the heat is too high.

8. Add the **chicken**. (This dish works well with chicken tikka, but just plain chicken is fine.) Stir.

9. If you like, lift the pan handle and tilt the pan to the gas to give it a little roasty flambé effect.

10. Add **gravy** to cover, and keep stirring. Turn the heat up and reduce it.

11. When it has the consistency that you like, stir in a good pinch of **coriander**. Done.

NOTES – Chicken jalfrezi

Chicken madras

This classic dish is one of the simplest but tastiest of them all. It's a fairly hot, no-frills dish with a tomato-based sauce. I like it with a hint of lemon.

....

- oil
- tomato puree
- *dipping*
- chilli powder
- (tandoori marinade)
- chicken
- gravy
- lemon (1 slice)
- coriander

Dipping

garlic and ginger puree

tandoori masala

curry powder

 salt

cumin

black or white pepper

....

1. Frying pan onto the stove, low heat.
2. Use 1 curry spoon of **oil.** (If you like it a bit more oily, OK, 2 curry spoons.)
3. Add 1 level curry spoon of **tomato puree** and stir.
4. *Dipping* – **ginger and garlic puree, tandoori masala, curry powder, salt, cumin, black or white pepper.**
5. Add a good ½ level curry spoon of **chilli powder.** Give it a good stir.
6. Now it's up to you. Some people like to add some tandoori marinade at this stage. You can experiment with this.
7. Add the **chicken.** Give it a good stir, making sure every piece is well coated. Turn the heat up slightly.
8. Add the **gravy** and a slice of **lemon.** Stir well while it reduces. Catch it at just the right moment – when it's at the consistency you like (see Dave's Tips).

9. Finally add the pinch of fresh, chopped **coriander** and stir again. Done.

Dave's Tips

1. Some restaurants like to use a commercial chilli sauce in this recipe. One I worked in always used Maggi chilli and garlic sauce. You could try your favourite brand.

2. To my mind this dish is ready when it smells just right, which is just a few moments after the gravy goes in. If you leave it to thicken too much, it loses that classic madras flavour and tastes more like a very hot, over-spiced bhuna. (But the sauce mustn't be runny. It should be thick enough – and there should be enough of it – to make a good 'mud pie' when you mix it with the rice on your plate.)

NOTES – Chicken madras

Chicken patia

This sweet and sour version of an Indian curry was probably invented by BIR chefs as an equivalent to the popular Chinese sweet and sour chicken. Almost every recipe in this book is a version of recipes found in cookbooks in India; this one is an exception.

....

- oil
- *dipping*
- chicken
- patia sauce (see page 38)
- gravy
- coriander

Dipping
garlic & ginger puree
cumin
chilli powder
salt
curry powder

....

1. **Oil** – 2 curry spoons – into the pan, with heat on medium.
2. *Dipping* – **garlic and ginger puree, cumin, chilli powder, salt,** and a scant dip of **curry powder**. Stir.
3. Add **chicken** and coat with the spices.
4. Add **patia sauce** – enough to give the chicken a good red gloss – then add enough **gravy** to cover the chicken.
5. Reduce until thick and then add **coriander** to garnish. The result should be a thick, sweet and sour dish.

NOTES – Chicken patia

Chicken rogan josh

Some restaurants like to add a final little touch to this dish – a cooked garnish which I'm sure you'll find very nice. The base for this one is tomato and yoghurt, with a little lemon or lime juice.

....

- oil
- garlic and ginger puree
- tomato puree
- *dipping*
- tandoori marinade
- chicken
- gravy
- coriander

    Optional garnish

    - oil
    - chopped onion
    - patia sauce
    - gravy

Dipping

tandoori masala

cumin powder

curry powder

salt

chilli powder

....

1. **Oil**, say 2 curry spoons, into the pan, lowish heat.
2. Add **garlic and ginger puree** (¼ curry spoon) and a good splash of **tomato puree** – at least a good ½ curry spoon. Stir.
3. *Dipping* – tandoori masala, cumin powder, curry powder, salt, chilli powder. Stir thoroughly.
4. Add 2 level curry spoons of **tandoori marinade** (which supplies the yoghurt). Stir.
5. In with the **chicken**. Stir.

6. Add the **gravy** – just enough to cover, and turn the heat up to reduce.

The optional garnish

Some curry houses like to add this. While the contents of the main pan are still reducing, in a separate small pan:

(i) Add **oil**, then a handful of **chopped onion** and 1 curry spoon of **patia sauce**. Stir.

(ii) Now add a little **gravy** and heat to reduce it – it should be quite red. Turn off heat.

Back to the main pan.

7. When the rogan josh has reached the desired consistency, add some **coriander**, then into the serving dish with it. (Pour the garnish over the top.) Done.

NOTES – Chicken rogan josh

South Indian garlic chilli chicken

This is quite similar to chicken tikka garlic chicken, although it's not cooked with chicken tikka. A lot of curry houses like to add one plum tomato from a tin.

....

- oil
- garlic (1 bulb)
- *dipping*
- chicken
- gravy
- chillies
- tomato (1 plum)
- coriander

Dipping

tomato puree

garlic & ginger puree

salt

curry powder

tandoori masala

chilli powder

....

1. Frying pan onto the stove, low heat.
2. Put in 1 curry spoon of **oil**.
3. Add ½ a peeled and sliced bulb of **garlic**. Turn the heat up slightly and keep stirring until the garlic turns light brown around the edges and then starts to get sticky on the spoon. Now reduce heat.
4. *Dipping* – **tomato puree, garlic and ginger puree, salt, curry powder, tandoori masala, chilli powder.**
5. **Chicken** in. Give it a good stir to make sure it all gets coated, heat not too high.
6. Then the **gravy**. Just to cover, then add a few glugs of **water**, perhaps ½ a cup, to give lashings of gravy juice.
7. Add whole **chillies** – you decide the amount.

8. Put the **tomatoes** into a bowl, select the best one and add to the pan. Stir it in gently so you don't break it up, and turn the heat down a little. As soon as the tomato is warmed through to the centre and simmering away, it's ready.

9. Sprinkle on the **coriander**, stir, and it's into the serving dish. Arrange the tomato nicely in the centre.

10. Now it's a repeat of the tarka. Rinse the current pan or take a small clean one, add plenty of **oil** and the rest of the **garlic**, heat turned to medium. Wait till it is dark brown on the edges and light brown towards the centre, at which time it will become sticky.

11. Immediately take the pan off the stove, and pour the contents over the top of the prepared dish. As you pour you'll hear that lovely 'Ssshh' as it hits the pan, and the aroma will fill the room…

Dave's Tips

1. When you add the gravy also add the juice from the tin of tomatoes. This dish needs plenty of sauce.
2. Mango chutney is a great addition to this dish and transforms it into a real BIR classic.

NOTES – South Indian garlic chilli chicken

Chicken tikka garlic chilli

Amongst curry aficionados this dish is one of the most highly regarded. OK, chicken tikka masala is probably the best known, but I think that's because when couples have take-out they tend to choose a dish both are happy with. In my experience the ladies' favourites are chicken tikka masala and chicken korma (neither of which I really regard as curries) because they usually prefer dishes that aren't too hot or spicy. The favourites for the guys tend to be chicken vindaloo and chicken tikka garlic chilli, and the latter seems to have everything you could ask of a curry dish. It's adaptable, too. Those that don't like it too hot can just push the chillies to the side of the plate. It has the chicken tikka base, and served with vegetable rice and garlic nan, well, to me it's almost unbeatable.

And, as you'll see, the garlic is cooked properly! For my money, the French chefs have got it wrong when it comes to cooking garlic.

....

- oil
- garlic (1 bulb)
- *dipping*
- (gravy)
- chicken tikka
- gravy
- chillies
- coriander

Dipping

tomato puree

garlic & ginger puree

salt

curry powder

chilli powder

tandoori masala

....

1. Frying pan onto the stove, low heat.

2. Add 1 curry spoon of **oil** and heat gently for a few minutes.

3. Add ½ the bulb of **garlic** (with the cloves peeled and sliced lengthwise).

4. Turn the heat up slightly. Cook and stir… *keep* cooking. What you'll notice after a while is that the garlic will start to go light brown around the outside, then later it will begin to get sticky and will stick to your curry spoon as you stir. When that happens, turn the heat right down – as low as it will go – and take the pan off the stove. It's time to do your dipping.

5. *Dipping* – **tomato puree, garlic and ginger puree, salt, curry powder, chilli powder, tandoori masala.**

   Pan back onto the stove, give it a stir. If it gets too hot then give it a ¼ ladle of gravy – it won't spoil the flavour. (Now you'll have that beautiful garlic aroma coming out of the pan.)

6. In with the **chicken tikka,** stir. Make sure you get each piece thoroughly coated.

7. When the chicken is coated, add the **gravy** – just enough to cover – and then a few glugs of **water** to thin it down. (Don't use extra gravy for thinning. All the flavour is already there, but you do want plenty of sauce.)

8. **Chillies** in (I use a handful): whole if you like it mild; sliced down the middle if you like it hot; and chopped into pieces if you like it HOT.

9. Cook it down until it gets to the consistency that you want, then empty the contents into the serving dish, sprinkle in some **coriander** and leave the dish to the side.

10. Rinse the pan (or get another), back onto the stove, low heat, and add **oil**. Don't be afraid to use plenty of oil for this one – 2 or even 3 curry spoons. (Canola is good. *Don't use ghee for this one.* Garlic and ghee aren't a happy combination – the garlic doesn't seem to infuse well into it.)

11. Add the remaining half of the **garlic.** (Just as we did with the tarka dahl – you are now making a tarka.) Give it a good stir. Now it's as for step 4.

When the garlic gets sticky to the spoon, turn the heat off and pour the whole contents of the pan over your serving dish.

Give it a little stir, and you're done – and ready to delight your guests.

Dave's Tips

1. At the end of stage 5, it's up to you. Some chefs add a few extras – chutney, tandoori marinade... but my advice is to just leave it be. The dish contains masses of flavours as it is, and you don't want to compromise them. The flavours are clean, they're right, so why muddy things?

2. Stage 8

The whole chillies won't add heat to the dish, but they will add their nice capsicum flavour. Those at the table who like their curry very mild can merely push the chillies to the side, while those that like it hot can chop them in.

NOTES – Chicken tikka garlic chilli

Chicken vindaloo

This is a chicken and potato dish in a hot tomato sauce. (It's similar to chicken madras, but it's quite a bit hotter.) *Aloo* is Indian for potato; there's Aloo gobi, Bombay aloo... But regardless of its name, some like this dish served without potatoes.

....

- oil
- **tomato puree**
- *dipping*
- **chilli powder**
- **(gravy)**
- **chicken**
- **(potatoes, pre-boiled)**
- **vinegar (or sliced lemon)**
- **chilli flakes**
- gravy
- **coriander (fresh, chopped)**

Dipping

garlic & ginger puree

tandoori masala

salt

curry powder

cumin

....

1. Frying pan onto the stove, low heat.
2. Add 1 curry spoon of **oil**.
3. Add **tomato puree** – a healthy 1-1½ curry spoons.
4. *Dipping* – **garlic and ginger puree, tandoori masala, salt, curry powder, cumin** and stir.
5. Add between ½ -1 curry spoon of **chilli powder** and *keep stirring*.
   If it gets too hot and starts to stick, in with a bit of gravy, and give it a good stir.
6. In with the **chicken** and the **potatoes** (if you've elected to use them) and stir well.

7. Add 1 capful of **vinegar** (your choice, although red wine vinegar is good with this recipe), or alternatively a slice of **lemon**, and give it a good stir.

8. Add 1 level curry spoon of **chilli flakes**; good stir.

9. Add the **gravy**, just enough to cover, turn the heat up, and keep heating and stirring until you have your desired consistency. Then it's into the serving dish.

10. Add a sprinkle of **coriander**, stir in, and serve.

Dave's Tips

1. Chilli flakes are available from your Asian grocer, and often from your supermarket. Seeds are incorporated with the flakes and it's one way of getting a good, hot, chilli flavour into a dish. However, as some brands are quite mild, you could instead grind some small, dried, red chillies – with their seeds – into the dish.

2. You could add lime pickles to the dipping, and I often replace the vinegar with a slice or two of lemon or lime.

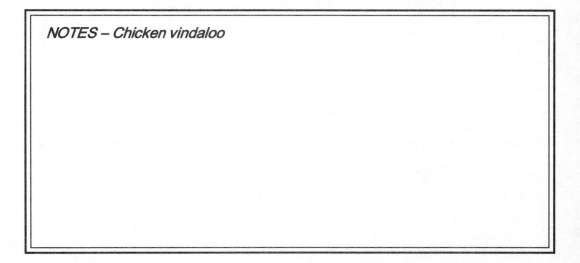

NOTES – Chicken vindaloo

BEEF and LAMB RECIPES

Beef or lamb achar pall

Pre-cooking the meat, as advised earlier, results in this being a very tasty and satisfying dish. Note that because you've used the gravy in the meat's preparation, this curry tends to be milder than chicken achar pall. However, you can adjust it to suit your taste with the addition of extra chilli flakes or ground chillies (see Dave's Tips).

....

- oil
- *dipping*
- tomato puree
- lime or mixed vegetable pickle
- chilli flakes (dried)
- (gravy)
- red and/or green pepper (handful)
- meat (700-800g, pre-cooked weight)
- gravy
- coriander (fresh, chopped)

Dipping

garlic & ginger puree

tandoori masala

curry powder

salt

chilli powder

cumin

....

1. **Oil** – 2 curry spoons into the pan and heat.
2. *Dipping* – garlic and ginger puree, tandoori masala, curry powder, salt, chilli powder, cumin.

   (Check the 'Dipping' notes, page 58, as needed.)
3. Add ½ a curry spoon of **tomato puree.**
4. In with the **lime** or **mixed vegetable pickle** – about a forkful, and stir. If you see any big lumps of pickle, use the spoon edge to cut them up against the side

of the pan. (Give the pan a good bang – it all adds to the effect.) Any small lumps can be left.

5. A level spoon of **dried chilli flakes**. Give it a stir. Turn the heat up slightly, but don't let it burn. If it starts to burn or stick, add a ¼ of a level curry spoon of gravy and keep stirring, keep stirring.

6. Add a handful of sliced **red and/or green pepper.**

7. Add the **beef** or **lamb** and stir to thoroughly coat it with the pan's contents.

8. Add **gravy**, just enough to cover the meat.

9. Give it a really good stir, reduce to the desired consistency, then add a large pinch of **coriander** and give it a good final stir. It's done and into the serving dish.

Dave's Tips

1. You might wish to add more oil if you find that the spices have absorbed most of it. You need to have enough oil to fry them, and it can always be skimmed off at the end.

2. You can add fresh chillies if you like, and for those that like it really hot, grind some very small, dried, red chillies – with their seeds – to a fine powder. When you add these even the most ardent fire-eater will be satisfied.

NOTES – Beef or lamb achar pall

Beef or lamb bhuna

This dish has a thick sauce, nice and red usually.

Good additions to the norm are tandoori marinade and just a touch of lemon. A pinch of ground fennel also enhances and personalises it.

....

- oil
- tomato puree
- *dipping*
- lemon juice (¼ squeeze)
- (tandoori marinade)
- beef/lamb
- gravy
- coriander

Dipping

garlic & ginger puree

tandoori masala

curry powder

chilli powder

salt

....

1. **Oil,** 1 curry spoon, into the pan, low heat.
2. Add 1 level curry spoon of **tomato puree,** stir. Turn the heat up slightly to get a nice, steady, but *not* vigorous bubble.
3. *Dipping* – **garlic and ginger puree, tandoori masala, curry powder, chilli powder, salt.**
   Stir away and let the aromas waft up.
4. Add just a tiny touch of **lemon juice,** say a ¼ of a squeeze.
5. A good option is adding ½ a level curry spoon of **tandoori marinade**. Give it a good stir.
6. In with the **beef** or **lamb** and get it all coated with the sauce.
7. Add enough **gravy** to just cover the meat. Turn the heat up a bit and keep it going until it's been reduced to a really thick sauce and the meat has a thick,

sticky coating.

8. Thirty seconds before you're ready to serve, throw in a good pinch of fresh **coriander** and stir.

Dave's Tips

As well as adding to the flavour, the tandoori marinade gives the meat an attractive pink colour.

NOTES – Beef or lamb bhuna

Beef or lamb danzak

Lamb danzak is one of my real favourites. When served with vegetables, rice and garlic nan you have a fully balanced meal: lentils and meat for protein; rice and bread for carbohydrates; vegetables (also in the gravy); and vitamins and nutrients in the spices and the pineapple.

I always have it vindaloo hot. Ahh – unbeatable!

Before making the dish, cook two heaped curry spoons of lentils, and let them cool. (If you'll be making this again in the near future, cook more and refrigerate the excess.)

....

- oil
- tomato puree
- *dipping*
- chilli powder
- (gravy)
- meat (see 'Quantities', p. 63)
- lentils (pre-cooked, cold, 2 heaped curry spoons)
- gravy
- pineapple juice
- pineapple (2 rings)
- coriander (fresh, chopped)

Dipping

garlic and ginger puree

salt

curry powder

tandoori masala

....

1. Pan on stove, low heat, add 1 full curry spoon of **oil**.
2. Add ½ a curry spoon of **tomato puree**.
3. *Dipping* – garlic and ginger puree, salt, curry powder, tandoori masala.
4. Now the **chilli powder**. How much is up to you – you're the cook.

Give it all a good stir. Turn the heat up a bit, and *keep stirring*.

If it starts to burn, add ¼ ladle of gravy and stir it in.

5. In with the **beef** or **lamb**, and make sure each piece gets a good coating.

6. Add 2 big heaped curry spoons of the **pre-cooked cold lentils.** Mix in, and mix again.

7. In with the **gravy**, just enough to cover, or even a bit less.

8. Add **pineapple juice** (2 curry spoons), and a couple of **pineapple** rings. They can be chopped or left whole to make it easier for those who really don't like pineapple. Turn the heat down.

9. When it's ready, dip forefinger and thumb into the chopped **coriander** and sprinkle it in. Give it a quick stir and it's done.

Dave's Tips

1. This one is notorious for burning. At step 6 onwards you've got to watch for that. Stir constantly, turn the heat down and just gently heat it through.

2. If, like me, you want your danzak to be vindaloo hot, at stage four, add either a quantity of vindaloo sauce (one or two curry spoons should be adequate) or a curry spoon of vinegar, one of tomato puree and one of either crushed chillies or extra hot chilli powder. Splendid.

NOTES – Beef or lamb danzak

Beef or lamb dopiazza

This is a very popular dish. The long cooking time of the onion sauce brings out the onion's natural sweetness. Because of this, and its mildness, it's a good one to give to your kids. When you do, if you intend to add chilli powder, don't add it at the dipping stage. Wait until the children have been served before stirring it in.

- oil
- tomato puree (¼ curry spoon)
- *dipping*
- beef/lamb
- onion sauce (1½ curry spoons)
- gravy
- coriander

Dipping

garlic & ginger puree

curry powder

salt

tandoori masala

(chilli powder)

1. Frying pan on stove, low flame. Put 1 curry spoon of **oil** into the pan and give it a bit of a stir.
2. Add **tomato puree** (only ¼ of a curry spoon), and stir.
3. *Dipping* – **garlic and ginger puree, curry powder, salt, tandoori masala, chilli powder**. Stir thoroughly.
4. Throw in the **beef** or **lamb** and get it all coated.
5. Now add the **onion sauce** (1½ curry spoons) and stir in well.
   Turn the heat up and give the pan a good vigorous fry. Tip the pan to flambé it. Impress your guests – bang and rattle the pan a bit (yes, just like in a curry house) and keep shaking, shaking.
6. Add the **gravy** – not too much, just enough to cover the meat. Remember,

you've already added onion sauce, and that contains gravy as well.

7. Keep it on a high heat, and when you've got your desired consistency, add a pinch of fresh, chopped **coriander**, mix, and it's done.

Dave's Tips

1. If you've been working your way through the recipes, you'll know about dipping. Details are on page 58. But briefly, dip the edge of the spoon lightly into each spice container in turn, tapping the contents into the pan each time.

2. Storing your spices in a 750 ml plastic container, such as those you buy your take-away in, allows for easy dipping. Forget teaspoons; this method is easier, faster, better.

NOTES – Beef or lamb dopiazza

Beef or lamb jalfrezi

This is a very versatile dish which can be transformed into many other dishes by the addition of a variety of other ingredients. For example, convert it to beef or lamb madras by adding half a curry spoon of tomato puree with the garlic and ginger puree, and a very thin slice of lemon or lime when you add the gravy. Alternatively, make a beef or lamb jalfrezi vindaloo by merely adding a curry spoon of vindaloo sauce. Or, convert it to a beef or lamb jalfrezi achari bhoona with the addition of half a forkful of lime pickle and then cooking until the gravy has reduced to a very thick consistency.

What all this means is that you can, if you wish, make four different dishes to please four different diners at the one meal. *This is one of the key features of the one pot cookery system.*

....

- oil
- tomato puree
- *dipping*
- (gravy)
- red & green peppers (small handful of each)
- chillies
- mango chutney
- beef/lamb
- gravy
- coriander

Dipping

tandoori masala

chilli powder

salt

garlic & ginger puree

curry powder

tandoori marinade

....

1. Put 1 curry spoon of **oil** into the pan and warm it.

2. Add **tomato puree** and stir.

3. *Dipping* – tandoori masala, chilli powder, salt, garlic and ginger puree,
   curry powder, tandoori marinade. Stir.

4. Keep stirring. You need to avoid any sticking at this point. If it wants to brown, add ¼ of a ladle of gravy.

5. Add a scant handful of each of **red and green pepper**, cut into strips.

6. Add whole **chillies**, and STIR.

7. Take up a little **mango chutney** on a fork, add, and stir again – the chutney will burn if the heat is too high.

8. Add the **beef** or **lamb**. Stir.

9. If you like, lift the pan handle and tilt the pan to the gas to catch and give it a little roasty flambé effect.

10. Add **gravy** to cover, and keep stirring. Turn the heat up and reduce the contents.

11. When it has the consistency that you like, stir in a good pinch of **coriander**. Done.

NOTES – Beef or lamb jalfrezi

Beef or lamb madras

This classic dish is one of the simplest but tastiest of them all. It's a no-frills, fairly hot dish with a tomato-based sauce, and I like it with a hint of lemon.

....

- oil
- tomato puree
- *dipping*
- chilli powder
- (tandoori marinade)
- beef/lamb
- gravy
- lemon (1 slice)
- coriander

Dipping

garlic & ginger puree

tandoori masala

curry powder

salt

cumin

black or white pepper

....

1. Frying pan onto the stove, low heat.
2. Add 1 curry spoon of **oil**. (If you like it a bit more oily, use 2 curry spoons.)
3. Add 1 level curry spoon of **tomato puree**, and stir well.
4. *Dipping* – **garlic and ginger puree, tandoori masala, curry powder, salt, cumin, black or white pepper.**
   Then add a good ½ level curry spoon of **chilli** powder. Give it a good stir.
5. At this point, it's up to you. Some people like to add some tandoori marinade now. You can experiment with this.
6. Add the **beef** or **lamb**, good stir, making sure every piece is well coated; turn heat up slightly.

7. Add the **gravy** and a thin slice of **lemon**. Give it a good stir while it reduces. Catch it at just the right moment – when it's at the consistency you like.

9. Finally, add the usual pinch of fresh **coriander** and stir again. Done.

Dave's Tips

1. Some restaurants like to use a commercial chilli sauce in this recipe. I worked in one that always used Maggi chilli and garlic sauce. You could try your favourite brand.

2. To my mind this dish is ready when it smells just right, which is just a few moments after the gravy goes in. If you leave it to thicken too much, it loses that classic madras flavour and instead tastes more like a very hot, over-spiced bhuna.

(But the sauce mustn't be runny. It should be thick enough – and there should be enough of it – to make a good 'mud pie' when you mix it with the rice on your plate.)

NOTES – Beef or lamb madras

Beef or lamb patia

This is a sweet and sour version of an Indian curry, probably invented by BIR chefs as an equivalent to the popular sweet and sour dish served in Chinese restaurants.

....

- oil
- *dipping*
- beef/lamb
- patia sauce (see page 38)
- gravy
- coriander

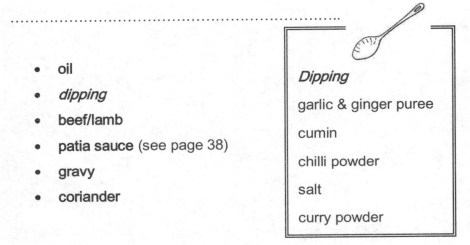

Dipping

garlic & ginger puree

cumin

chilli powder

salt

curry powder

....

1. **Oil** – 2 curry spoons – into the pan, with heat on medium.
2. *Dipping* – garlic and ginger puree, cumin, chilli powder, salt, and a *scant* dip of curry powder. Stir.
3. Add the **beef** or **lamb** and coat with the spices.
4. Add **patia sauce** – enough to give the meat a good red gloss – then add enough **gravy** to cover the meat.
5. Reduce until thick, then add **coriander.** The result should be a thick, sweet and sour dish.

NOTES – Beef or lamb patia

Beef or lamb rogan josh

Some restaurants like to add an extra touch to this dish – a cooked garnish which I'm sure you'll find very nice. The base for this one is tomato and yoghurt, with a little lemon or lime juice.

....

- oil
- garlic and ginger puree
- tomato puree
- *dipping*
- tandoori marinade
- beef/lamb
- gravy
- coriander

    Optional garnish

    - oil
    - chopped onion
    - patia sauce
    - gravy

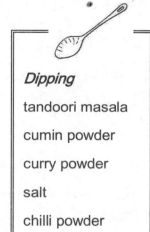

Dipping

tandoori masala

cumin powder

curry powder

salt

chilli powder

....

1. **Oil,** say 2 curry spoons, into the pan, lowish heat.
2. Add **garlic and ginger puree** (¼ of a curry spoon) and a good splash of **tomato puree** – at least a good ½ curry spoon. Stir.
3. *Dipping* – tandoori masala, cumin powder, curry powder, salt, chilli powder and stir thoroughly.
4. Add 2 level curry spoons of **tandoori marinade** (which supplies the yoghurt). Stir.
5. In with the **beef** or **lamb**. Stir.

6. Add the **gravy** – just enough to cover, and turn the heat up to reduce.

    The optional garnish

    Some curry houses like to add this. While the contents of the main pan are still reducing, in a separate small pan:

    (i) Add **oil**, then a handful of **chopped onion** and 1 curry spoon of **patia sauce.** Stir.

    (ii) Now add a little **gravy** and heat to reduce. It should be quite red. Turn off heat.

    Back to the main pan.

7. When the rogan josh has reached the desired consistency, add some fresh **coriander**, then into the serving dish with it. (Pour the optional garnish over the top.)

    Done.

NOTES – Beef or lamb rogan josh

South Indian garlic chilli beef or lamb

Quite similar to tikka garlic chilli, although it's not cooked with meat tikka and a lot of curry houses like to add a plum tomato.

....

- oil
- garlic (1 bulb)
- *dipping*
- beef/lamb
- gravy
- chillies
- tomato (1 plum)
- coriander

Dipping

tomato puree

garlic & ginger puree

salt

curry powder

tandoori masala

chilli powder

....

1. Frying pan onto the stove, low heat.
2. Add 1 curry spoon of **oil**.
3. Add ½ the peeled and sliced bulb of **garlic**. Turn the heat up slightly and keep stirring until the garlic turns light brown around the edges and then starts to get sticky on the spoon.
4. *Dipping* – tomato puree, garlic and ginger puree, salt, curry powder, tandoori masala, chilli powder.
5. **Beef** or **lamb** in. Give it a good stir to make sure it all gets coated, heat not too high.
6. Then the **gravy**. Just to cover the meat, then add a few glugs of **water**, perhaps ½ a cup, to give lashings of gravy juice.
7. Add whole **chillies** – you decide the amount.

8. Put the **tomatoes** into a bowl. Select the best one and add it to the pan. Stir it in gently so you don't break it up, and turn the heat down a bit. As soon as the tomato is warmed through, it's ready.

9. Sprinkle on the **coriander**, stir, and into the serving dish. Arrange the tomato nicely in the centre.

10. Now it's a repeat of the tarka. Rinse the current pan or take a small clean one, plenty of **oil**, the rest of the **garlic** and heat on medium. Wait till it's dark brown on the edges and light brown towards the centre, when it will become sticky.

11. Immediately take the pan off the stove, and pour the contents over the top of the prepared dish. As you pour you'll hear that lovely 'Ssshh' as it hits the pan, and the aroma will fill the room…

Dave's Tips

1. When you add the gravy also add the juice from the tin of tomatoes – you need plenty of sauce for this one.

2. Mango chutney is a great addition to this dish, transforming it into a BIR classic.

NOTES – South Indian garlic chilli beef or lamb

Beef or lamb tikka garlic chilli

Amongst curry aficionados this dish is one of the most highly regarded. It's also adaptable, and those that don't like it too hot can just push the chillies to the side of the plate. There's the tikka flavour, and served with vegetable rice and garlic nan, well, to me it's almost unbeatable. (See page 42 for the beef or lamb tikka recipe.)

And, as you'll see, the garlic is cooked properly! For my money, the French chefs have got it wrong when it comes to cooking garlic.

....

- oil
- garlic (1 bulb)
- *dipping*
- (gravy)
- beef/lamb tikka (see p.42)
- gravy
- chillies
- coriander

Dipping

tomato puree

garlic & ginger puree

salt

curry powder

chilli powder

tandoori masala

....

1. Frying pan onto the stove, low heat.
2. Add 1 curry spoon of **oil** and heat gently for a few minutes.
3. Now add half the bulb of **garlic**. (It's been peeled and sliced lengthwise.)
4. Turn the heat up slightly. Cook and stir, keep cooking. What you'll notice after a while is that the garlic will start to go light brown around the outside, then later it will begin to get sticky – it will stick to your curry spoon as you stir. When that happens, turn the heat right down – as low as it

will go – then take the pan off the stove, and it's time to do your dipping.

5. *Dipping* – tomato puree, garlic and ginger puree, salt, curry powder, chilli powder, tandoori masala.

   Pan back on the stove, give it a stir. If it gets too hot then give it that ¼ ladle of gravy – it won't spoil the flavour. (Now you'll be getting that beautiful garlic aroma coming out of the pan.)

6. In with the **meat**. Stir, making sure you get each piece thoroughly coated.

7. When the meat is cooked, add the **gravy** – just enough to cover – and then a few glugs of **water** to thin it down. (Don't use extra gravy for thinning. All the flavour is already there, but you still want plenty of sauce.)

8. **Chillies** in (I use a handful): whole if you like it mild, sliced down the middle if you like it hot, and chopped into pieces if you like it HOT.

9. Cook it down until it gets to the consistency that you want, then empty the contents into the serving dish, sprinkle in some **coriander** and leave the dish to the side.

10. Rinse the pan (or get another), back onto the stove, low heat, oil into the curry spoon and into the pan. Don't be afraid to use plenty of oil for this – 1, 2, or even 3 spoons. (Canola is good. Don't use ghee for this one. Garlic and ghee aren't a happy combination – the garlic doesn't seem to infuse well into it.)

11. Add the rest of the **garlic,** the other half. (Just as we did with the tarka dahl – you are now making a tarka.) Give it a good stir. Now it's as for step 4.

    When the garlic gets sticky to the spoon, turn the heat off and pour the whole contents of the pan over your serving dish.

    Give it a little stir, and you're done – and ready to delight your guests.

Dave's Tips

1. At the end of step 5, it's up to you. Some chefs add a few extras – chutney, tandoori marinade... but my advice is to just leave it be. The dish is full of flavours as it is, and you don't want to compromise those. They are clean, they're right, so why muddy things?

2. Step 8

The whole chillies won't add heat to the dish, but they *will* add their nice capsicum flavour. Those at the table who like their curry mild will merely push the chillies to the side, while those that like it hot can chop them in.

NOTES – Beef or lamb tikka garlic chilli

Beef or lamb vindaloo

This is a beef/lamb and potato dish in a hot tomato sauce. (It's similar to beef/lamb madras, but it's quite a bit hotter.) *Aloo* is Indian for potato; there's Aloo gobi, Bombay aloo... But regardless of its name, some prefer this dish served without potatoes.

....

- oil
- tomato puree
- *dipping*
- chilli powder
- (gravy)
- beef/lamb
- (potatoes, pre-boiled)
- vinegar (or sliced lemon)
- chilli flakes
- gravy
- coriander

Dipping

garlic & ginger puree

tandoori masala

salt

curry powder

cumin

....

1. Frying pan onto the stove, low flame.
2. Add 1 curry spoon of **oil**.
3. **Tomato puree** – a healthy 1-1½ curry spoons.
4. *Dipping* – **garlic and ginger puree**, **tandoori masala**, **salt**, **curry powder**, **cumin** and stir.
5. Add between ½ -1 curry spoon of **chilli powder** and *keep stirring*. If it gets a bit hot and starts to stick, in with a bit of gravy and give it a good stir.
6. In with the **beef** or **lamb**, stir thoroughly, and add potatoes if you are using them.

7. Add a capful of **vinegar** (your choice, although red wine vinegar is good with this recipe) or alternatively a slice of lemon. Good stir.

8. Add a level curry spoon of **chilli flakes**. Good stir.

9. Add the **gravy** – just enough to cover – turn the heat up, and keep heating and stirring until you have your desired consistency. Then it's into the serving dish.

10. Sprinkle of **coriander**, stir in, and serve.

Dave's Tips

1. Chilli flakes are available from your Asian grocer, and often from your supermarket. Seeds are incorporated with the flakes and it's one way of getting a good, hot, chilli flavour into a dish. However, as some brands are quite mild, you could instead grind some small, dried, red chillies – with their seeds – into the dish.

2. You could add lime pickles to the dipping, and I often use lemon or lime in place of the vinegar.

NOTES – Beef or lamb vindaloo

PRAWN DISHES

These are the least ordered dishes, perhaps because the curry flavours tend to overpower the more delicate seafood flavours. I've included just a few milder dishes that are less likely to do this but, of course, you can experiment with any seafood. Marinate for a short time in tandoori marinade, for example, or brush fresh prawns with garlic and ginger puree prior to cooking on a grill or BBQ. Delicious! Fresh prawns are desirable as they have a stronger flavour than frozen. Peel, de-vein and cook in just a little oil, or boiling salted water, until pink.

Prawn bhuna

This dish has a thick sauce, nice and red usually, which suits the prawns.

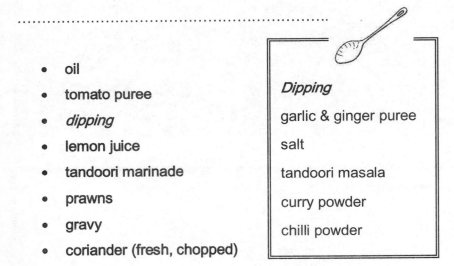

- oil
- tomato puree
- *dipping*
- lemon juice
- tandoori marinade
- prawns
- gravy
- coriander (fresh, chopped)

Dipping

garlic & ginger puree

salt

tandoori masala

curry powder

chilli powder

1. Curry spoon, fill it with **oil**, into the pan on low heat.
2. Add 1 level curry spoon of **tomato puree,** stir, then turn the heat up slightly to get nice, steady but *not* vigorous bubble.
3. *Dipping* – **garlic and ginger puree, salt**, then a *light* dip of each of
   tandoori masala, curry powder, chilli powder, and stir in.

4. Squeeze in the juice of half a **lemon.**

5. Add a ¼ of a level curry spoon of **tandoori marinade**, and give it a good stir.

6. In with the **prawns,** getting them all nicely coated.

7. Add the **gravy** – just enough to cover the prawns. Turn the heat up a bit and keep it going until it's been reduced to a really thick sauce and the prawns have a thick, sticky coating.

8. Thirty seconds before you're ready to serve, throw in a good pinch of coriander and stir.

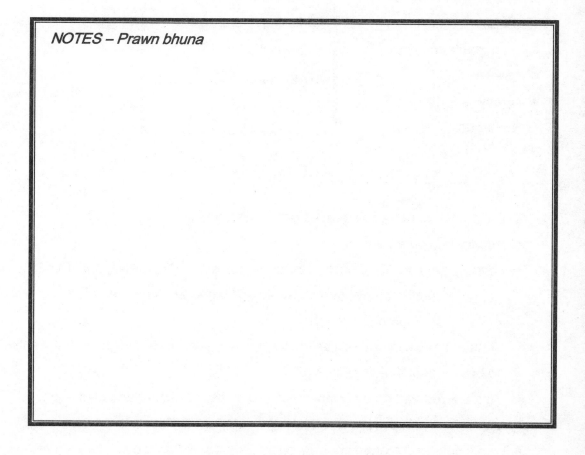

NOTES – Prawn bhuna

Prawn jalfrezi

This dish has a variety of flavours, but they all need to be delicate in order that they don't mask the flavour of the prawns, so don't dip too heavily.

....

- oil
- **tomato puree**
- *dipping*
- (gravy)
- **red & green pepper**
- chillies
- **mango chutney**
- **prawns**
- gravy
- coriander

Dipping

tandoori masala

chilli powder

garlic & ginger puree

curry powder

tandoori marinade

salt

....

1. Put 1 curry spoon of **oil** into the pan and warm it.
2. Add **tomato puree** and stir.
3. *Dipping* – a *light* dip of each of **tandoori masala, chilli powder, garlic** and **ginger puree, curry powder** and **tandoori marinade** and a standard dip of **salt.**
4. Stir and keep stirring. You want to avoid any sticking at this point. If it wants to brown, add ¼ ladle of gravy.
5. Add the **red** and **green pepper**, cut into strips – a scant handful of each.
6. Add whole **chillies** (you decide the amount) and STIR.
7. Take up a little **mango chutney** on a fork, add and stir again. Be careful –

the chutney will burn if the heat is too high.

8. Add the **prawns** and stir to get them all nicely coated.

9. Add **gravy** to cover the prawns, and keep stirring. Turn the heat up and reduce the mix.

10. When it has the consistency that you like, stir in a good pinch of **coriander**. Done.

NOTES – Prawn jalfrezi

Prawn madras

This classic dish is simple and tasty. It's a fairly hot no-frills dish with a tomato-based sauce. We'll cut back the usual half curry spoon of chilli powder to just a healthy dip. Use a good dash of lemon.

....

- oil
- **tomato puree**
- *dipping*
- **(tandoori marinade)**
- **prawns**
- **gravy**
- **lemon (squeeze and a slice)**
- **coriander**

Dipping

garlic & ginger puree

tandoori masala

curry powder

 salt

cumin

black or white pepper

chilli powder

....

1. Frying pan onto the stove, low heat.
2. Add 1 curry spoon of **oil.**
3. Add 1 level spoon of **tomato puree.** Good stir.
4. *Dipping* – **garlic and ginger puree, tandoori masala, curry powder, salt, cumin, black or white pepper,** then a good, healthy dip of **chilli powder.**
   Give it a good stir.
5. At this point, it's up to you. Some people like to add a little tandoori marinade at this stage. You can experiment with this.
6. Add the **prawns,** and give everything a good stir, making sure every prawn is well-coated. Turn the heat up slightly.
7. Add the **gravy,** stir again and as you stir select the consistency you like – it

will reduce and you've got to catch it at just the right moment.

8. When you're getting close, first add a good squeeze, and then a thin slice, of **lemon** and stir.

9. Add a pinch of **coriander**, a light final stir, and it's done.

Dave's Tips

1. Some restaurants like to use a commercial chilli sauce in this recipe. I worked in one that always used Maggi chilli and garlic sauce. You could try your favourite brand.

2. Don't reduce this dish too much. It should be ready just a few minutes after the gravy goes in. (But the sauce mustn't be runny. It should be thick enough – and there should be enough of it – to make a good 'mud pie' when you mix it with the rice on your plate.)

NOTES – Prawn madras

EXTRAS

Menu for Six

Friends coming over for dinner? There are obviously almost limitless menu possibilities but here's one of my favourites.

Starters: onion bhajis with dip

Mains:

- ❖ chicken tikka garlic chilli
- ❖ chicken madras
- ❖ lamb danzak

Accompaniments:

- ❖ palau rice and chapattis or battora
- ❖ a bowl of green salad with cherry tomatoes and slices of avocado
  (It's pleasing to both the eye and the palate.)

To finish: a dessert of your choosing, if you wish.

....

Each spice adds its own flavour, but it's not always essential to include <u>all</u> those listed in the ingredients.

In fact if you omit a spice in error, you may even stumble across a very pleasing result. When experimenting, consider not only what you could add, but also what you could leave out (but never the salt).

As long as you can keep the meals warm, a rest time definitely enhances the flavours.

Finished cooking? Let the meals rest a few minutes before serving.

Curry for Kids

In general

Most kids enjoy a curry provided it's not hot. Curries are tasty, colourful and healthy, and can easily be adapted to an individual child's taste. Remember the comment on page 37 about making a mild chicken bhuna for one guest and changing it to a hot chicken bhuna vindaloo merely by adding some vindaloo sauce? Similar simple methods can be used any time you're cooking for your family or friends and their children. For example, if I'm cooking a dish which contains chillies for my family, I either leave them whole and serve them just to the adults, or I cook them in a second pan and add them to the dish only after the child has been served.

Child friendly dishes

Onion bhajis are always a big hit with kids, as are dips and most of the fried snacks. Follow these with a mild main dish such as kebabs, chicken dopiazza or chicken pakora, served with a green salad and Palau rice or a bread. Finish with a fruit salad and you have provided a tasty and healthy meal.

A recipe for chicken pakora is not given elsewhere in the book, and so…

Chicken pakora

To 1 cup of **self-raising flour** add a pinch of **salt** and a dip of each of **cumin, curry powder, tandoori masala, coriander** and **turmeric**. Now add a pinch of whole **cumin seeds**, and a teaspoon of **baking powder**.

Combine all and mix with enough **water** to get a smooth mix the consistency of thick soup. Dip pre-cooked chicken portions (steamed or fried) into the mix, then cook in hot oil until the batter turns golden brown. Serve with a dip (see page 68).

Vegetarian dishes

It's easy to adjust any of the recipes listed in this book to make them vegetarian – simply leave out the meat and in its place add whatever vegetables you like. (Frozen mixed vegetables are used by most restaurants but at home, fresh is the way to go – provided the vegetables really are fresh and not days old. On the occasions when truly fresh veggies are difficult to obtain, remember that snap frozen vegetables are highly nutritious.)

As for specific vegetarian dishes, *vegetable biryani* is discussed below, while the recipe for *mixed vegetable curry* is given in 'Side Dishes', and see pages 9 and 10 for *tarka dhal*. The *gravy* itself is, of course, vegetarian.

Biryani

This is a dish of a thousand variations, and one you can freely experiment with. Basically, it is rice combined with almost anything else – vegetables alone, or vegetables with chicken, meat or seafood. It is sometimes cooked in an oven, sometimes in a pan.

Vegetable biryani

Having prepared palau rice (see page 44) the day before, follow the usual steps – **oil** into the pan or wok, heat, then add just a scant dip (see page 58) of each of the usual dippings (**garlic and ginger puree, curry powder, salt, tandoori masala, tandoori marinade** and **cumin,** and include **tomato puree**).

Throw in your choice of chopped **assorted vegetables** and enough **gravy** to almost cover them. Heat the mixture and then reduce it until the pan is almost dry.

Use the curry spoon to sprinkle in cold **palau rice**. Invert the spoon and get it into the wok, scraping and mixing while shaking the wok. Continue until the rice and vegetables are mixed thoroughly. (If you're using a non-stick pan – which is good for this dish – you'll naturally be using a wooden spoon.)

And there's the vegetable biryani. It's that simple. (Restaurant chefs don't have the time for alternating the layers of rice and vegetables as is the tradition in India.) Some nice additions are raisins, butter beans, potatoes, cauliflower, chick peas, cabbage, and thinly sliced fennel (which is particularly nice).

Vegetable biryani is a great dish to experiment with.

Because it's possible to use a wide variety of vegetables, spices, quantities and additions in this dish, it provides an exceptionally rich opportunity for experimentation.

The Indian restaurant kitchen

It's time for a look behind the scenes of a BIR kitchen. Who is it manned by and what goes on in there?

There could be ten to fifteen chefs, each with their own specific tasks. At a well-patronised restaurant the chefs might knock out two to three hundred meals a night.

There's always someone peeling onions. It could be any one of the team from the first, second, or tandoori chefs to one of the waiters, although it's usually one of the drivers or dishwashers. The onions are peeled and thrown into a really big 50-60 litre stock pot. When full, the pot is moved over to one of the prep tables, where the onions are chopped and then placed with the other pots of vegetables ready for the gravy.

The lay-out

All the Indian restaurant kitchens I've been in have been laid out as follows.

To enter the kitchen from the restaurant, the staff walk into a small lobby where coats and the like are hung, and then turn right, into the kitchen. This means customers can't see directly in. As the waiters enter the kitchen they drop any dishes onto the draining board, although sometimes there's a hatch in the lobby wall, and the dishes are dropped straight in, adding to the general racket. There's the draining board, main sink, then another little sink, the tandoor oven in the corner, the chef's preparation area, stoves and deep fryers, and the big plate warmer cupboard.

Orders are put where the chef likes them – on the counter near the stove, above the 'hot cupboard' where the plates are kept warm. He prepares the orders and pops the dishes into the cupboard until the diners are done with starters. And that's another little trick. They like to have a dish in the warmer for about ten

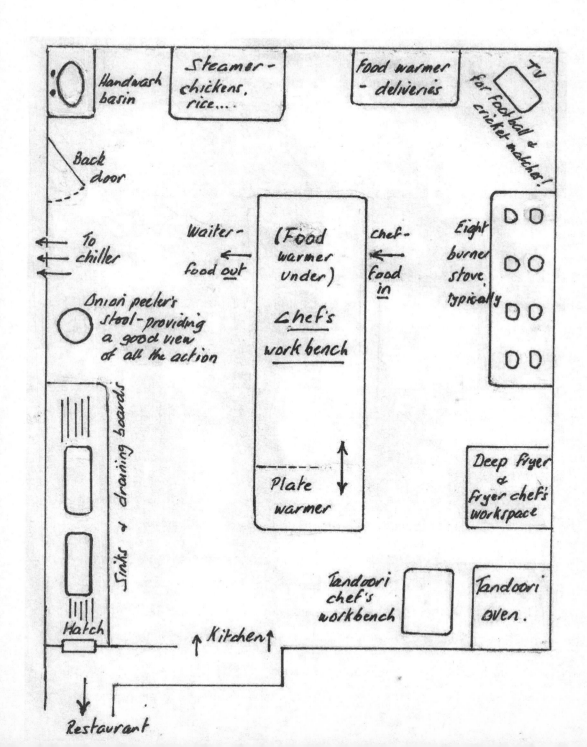

minutes to let the curry rest, and give the flavours time to blend. I'm convinced the rest period helps. So let's use this method ourselves. After you've cooked your curry, put it aside for a few minutes – in a metal container if there's no warming tray available, or on an electric hob if you've got one.

The eight burner stove is operated by the head chef. If there's a second chef he'll have a four burner stove. (Quite often these two won't share their secrets with each other.) The second chef may be responsible for only chicken tikka masala and one or two other dishes, while the head chef does all the remaining stove prepared dishes.

Then you have the fryer chef dealing with the onion bhajis, pakoras, samosas, shami kebabs and usually most of the starters, so he's got quite a lot to do. Naturally he's also responsible for the oil used to cook the fried side dishes because that goes into the gravy.

The tandoori chef deals with chicken tikkas, nan breads, tandoori prawns and sheekh kebabs. The green salads are prepared earlier in the day by anyone available.

The atmosphere

Especially on a busy Friday or Saturday night, there are two distinct and diametrically opposed atmospheres, pre-first meal and post-first meal.

At 4:55 pm the kitchen staff is working in dead silence (unless there's a football or cricket match on). At about 5 pm the first order might come in. After it's eaten, the waiter drops that first set of collected dishes with a 'Bang!' onto the draining board, and it's constant NOISE from then on.

The noise comes from everywhere – there are chefs banging and scraping pans, doors slamming, waiters dropping the dirty dishes onto the draining board and others rushing about shouting, 'Where are the starters for table 14?" or "Where's the nan for table 10?" I used to think it was a bit like being in a war zone. The noise is constant until hours later when, after the last customers have gone, the racket suddenly ceases and you breathe a sigh of relief.

The hierarchy

Naturally, the owners are at the top. Whichever one is on duty is generally walking around, greeting those customers he recognizes (which he can often do after their first visit). You'll be welcomed, looked after, and perhaps given a free drink if you're a regular client. When in the kitchen they oversee the whole operation. They don't take much notice of the drivers, which I was grateful for, since it worked to my advantage in my undercover role. The owners also work the till. Often, their sons will be working front of house, if they're in their late teens or older, but otherwise they'll be in the kitchen, learning the trade from the bottom up.

Out front are the waiters, of course. Incidentally, they are not allowed to handle or even carry money on their persons. If you tip your friendly waiter, the money will end up in a box by the till, I'm afraid, and that's possibly the last the waiter will see of it. That's the way it's been in all the restaurants I've worked in anyway. In one restaurant, the tip money was used to pay the waiters' wages.

After the owner and family, the next in the hierarchy is 'the man' – that one guy in the kitchen who can do everything, who knows it all. He's often Bangladeshi, and a number of the staff will probably be from the same village. He would have been a respected person with an established reputation back home, and they will trust him implicitly. He doesn't have a job title – although he's like a manager – but he can cover for anyone who is off sick or who has an immigration problem. He's a friend of everyone, including the drivers. He hears everything and his eyes are everywhere.

The first chef is next, and after *him* the social standings can get a bit blurred.

Sittings

There can be up to five sittings a day. Staff usually turn up at the restaurant at about 11 am to get ready for the midday opening.

The first sitting is lunch from noon to 2 pm. Often there's a special offer available, perhaps £5 for curry and rice. Restaurants then normally close from 2 to 5 pm, and staff get a well-earned rest before the war zone atmosphere starts at 5 pm.

Second sitting is from 5 to 7 pm.

Third – from 7 to 9 pm.

Fourth – from 9 to 11 pm.

Fifth is the late sitting after everybody's been out, had a good time and perhaps got a bit drunk. Some of these sittings go on past midnight, although the doors are sometimes shut then to stop others coming in. But once you're in, you're in, and some café restaurants stay open till 4 or 5 am. The chefs would have long gone by then, of course; once the last meal is cooked and the big tidy-up is finished it's off home for a rest before the 11 am start the following day.

Overall, the busiest time is from about 6:30 to 9:30 pm, straddling three sessions, and it's busy again after the pubs shut.

In a busy restaurant that has made its name, most sittings are full on most days of the week. In lesser known ones, Monday through to Wednesday can be pretty quiet.

CURRY AND HEALTH

The diet – health connection

There's good reason to question everything we eat because although we eat the foods we like, we also need to consider the effect that our food has on our health. Well, curry lovers, you're in luck, because the food *you* like is considered to be very good for you.

Support for this notion is gained by investigating the health of the nations in which curry forms a substantial part of the diet. Before India's economic surge pushed more of its population into the middle class bracket (leading to a move away from their traditional diet), its heart disease and cancer rates were among the world's lowest. For example, an American study in 2003 reported that the rates of colon and prostate cancers for Indian males were less than 5 individuals per 100,000 for both diseases compared to 41 and 105 respectively for United States males.

We have to be cautious, of course, in assuming that the Indian diet – and specifically the consumption of curry – is clearly linked to the health of its people, as other factors also contribute to it.

For example, it has been suggested that our genetic make-up plays a part, and that may well be true to a degree. This used to be proposed as a likely explanation for the low occurrence of heart disease amongst the Japanese – until studies showed that long term Japanese immigrants in North America, after years of consuming typical Western foods, suffered essentially the same rates of heart disease and cancer as Americans.

The 1975-2000 Okinawa Program found that the people of this Japanese island, which boasts the greatest number of centenarians in the world, owe their good health and longevity to their lifestyle and diet. This also lends considerable weight to the belief that it is these factors, not genetics, that are of primary importance.

The overall evidence is clear enough and, as a result, the link between good diet and good health has been accepted by mainstream science and medicine for decades. Certainly, the conclusion that diet has a big impact on health seems beyond argument. The adage that you are what you eat holds good.

The health benefits of curry

Each curry recipe includes a number of different spices, and spices are also part of both the 'core preparations' and the frequently used curry powder. All curry powders contain turmeric, most have coriander, cumin, and fenugreek, as well as any number of aniseed, cardamom, chillies, cinnamon, cloves, coriander, fennel, garlic, ginger, mustard seed, nutmeg/mace, pepper…

This prompts us to take a closer look at the typical components of curry dishes, the spices, to assess their health benefits, and upon investigation, we get a 100% positive result! It seems that every one of the spices normally used in curries has distinct health benefits, and in the following pages these are listed in some detail.

In addition to the spices, the gravy, the added vegetables and the other ingredients of curries are also high in food value.

And there's a general health property of curry that may surprise. A common perception is that although it's a great dish, it's not so good for the stomach. Yet nothing could be further from the truth. While a hot curry would not be recommended for someone suffering from diarrhoea, almost every curry spice has positive digestive properties.

The health benefits of spices – fact or fantasy?

A glance at the following list shows that some of the benefits attributed to certain spices seem extravagant, and such 'snake oil' reputations tend to make us sceptical. Rightly so, and a few of the claims from the past are certainly doubtful –

too many are supposed aphrodisiacs, for example (although perhaps rude good health leads to rude feelings!). But despite this, two points should be kept in mind.

Firstly, the health benefits of these plants have been the focus of a growing amount of recent research, and the findings have often supported the folklore. Many of the reputed benefits listed below are now either accepted by mainstream medicine, or considered well worthy of further investigation. Secondly, curry spices are usually derived from seeds or flower buds, the concentrated parts of plants. As a seed has to contain all that is initially needed for the plant to survive, regardless of the quality of the soil it finds itself in, it is not unexpected that it should contain a wide range of nutrient groups, and that these in turn should have wide ranging impacts on human health.

In the final event, you'll have to use your own judgment, or do some further reading and research. But overall, if a particular food has developed a long-standing reputation as being beneficial, and recent findings have supported some of its claims to fame, I'm prepared to accept its value in general terms even if I'm not necessarily convinced of all the particular claims.

How to use the list of spices and their benefits

The following list can be used in two ways.

You can look through it to see what health benefits a specific spice provides, or skim through it to locate spices that may be beneficial for particular medical conditions. Most of us know of someone with Type 2 diabetes, for example, and a quick check of the list reveals that one of cinnamon's many beneficial effects is improved utilization of sugar.

How is each spice assessed?

Each spice is assessed according to three criteria – the nutrients and minerals it contains, the extent of the scientific interest it has attracted, and its reputed benefits.

Nutrients and minerals

As the phytonutrient field is complex, only those nutrients which are more commonly known are mentioned, and only those minerals which are present in notably high amounts are listed. (As a result, some of the spices, such as cumin and fenugreek, although jam-packed with goodness, have only a few nutrients and minerals listed. So don't be too quick to dismiss a spice because of this.)

The health benefits of each individual mineral or nutrient (or the elements they contain) are not specified, as it is beyond the scope of this book. However, the benefits of many of them are widely known.

(Selenium, though, may be less well-known and as it is an essential trace element it's worthwhile at this stage to record its benefits. Research suggests it plays a part as an anti-inflammatory in diseases such as rheumatoid arthritis, it enhances the immune response, counteracts some viral infections, is essential for successful reproduction, is an antioxidant and possibly protects against cancers, particularly prostrate.)

Reputed benefits

Often, only a *general* property of a nutrient or mineral may be listed without detailing its specific health benefits. (For example, 'antioxidant' may be listed but its likely implications – reduction of free radical formation and hence reduced cancer and LDL problems – may not be.) Because of this, specific benefits commonly attributed to some of the foods may not be recorded.

Scientific interest

The degree of interest and investigation by the science community gives an indication of the likelihood that the benefits listed are based on recent studies rather than being mere folklore. (Although 'mere folklore' has been shown on many occasions to have sound substance.)

The number of recent studies undertaken (sometimes of the individual spices, more frequently of their active components) was determined by a Google search.

Certainly, only a small proportion of these studies would have been rigorous and peer reviewed, but at least the number gives an indication of the interest the various spices have attracted and so it was used as the basis for ranking. Due to the unreliability of the method, reservations about its accuracy are appropriate.

The rankings used to indicate the degree of scientific interest are: 'extensive', 'considerable', 'moderate' and 'limited'.

THE SPICES

In alphabetical order, the spices are…

Aniseed, anise

Nutrients and minerals: vitamins A, C and K, choline, selenium, calcium

Scientific interest: moderate

Reputed benefits: 'potently therapeutic, warming and enlivening the body'; stimulates circulation (hence could have migraine and blood pressure benefits); good for indigestion, flatulence, nausea, vomiting, colic; bactericide; recommended for bronchial complaints

Cardamom

Nutrients and minerals: vitamin C, dietary fibre, calcium, potassium, zinc, iron, manganese

Scientific interest: limited

Reputed benefits: antispasmodic; cleanses kidney and bladder; cures bad breath; detoxifies body of caffeine; improves circulation; improves digestion (relieves flatulence, stimulates appetite and metabolism)

Chillies

Nutrients and minerals:	capsaicin, vitamins A, C and K, dietary fibre, iron
Scientific interest:	limited
Reputed benefits:	reduced insulin required by Type 2 diabetics; aids digestion; antibacterial; antifungal; analgesic (capsaicin triggers release of endorphins); causes cancer cell death in rats; cuts cholesterol (assists in controlling LDL); improves circulation by dilating the blood vessels (hence can be used against cluster headaches, migraine); increases metabolism (hence a weight loss agent); breaks up congestion

Cinnamon

Nutrients and minerals:	dietary fibre, high iron content, good manganese and calcium
Scientific interest:	extensive
Reputed benefits:	a natural preservative; increases the ability of insulin to metabolize sugar, regulates sugar; lowers LDL cholesterol and triglycerides; its anti-clotting properties thin the blood, improve circulation, help prevent strokes; anti-inflammatory; powerful antioxidant; stops some medication resistant yeast infections; may slow proliferation of leukaemia and lymphoma cancer cells; may boost cognitive function and memory; relieves arthritis; digestive assistance (reduces flatulence, nausea, diarrhoea); helps protect against colon cancer

Cloves

Nutrients and minerals:	Omega-3 and vitamin K, manganese

Scientific interest:	moderate
Reputed benefits:	antibacterial; antifungal; antiseptic; anaesthetic (hence toothache remedy); cures bad breath; digestive assistance (relieves flatulence and promotes good digestion); improves circulation; effective in the digestive tract cancers studied; lowers triglycerides and LDL cholesterol

Coriander

Nutrients and minerals:	dietary fibre, flavinoids, iron, manganese
Scientific interest:	moderate
Reputed benefits:	antioxidant; relieves bloating and irritable bowel syndrome; acts in a similar manner to insulin, hence assists in diabetes; reduces anxiety; detoxifier (mercury, lead and other metals); reduces LDL cholesterol

Cumin

Nutrients and minerals:	high iron content, manganese
Scientific interest:	moderate
Reputed benefits:	anti-inflammatory; aids digestion; detoxifier; excellent for respiratory conditions (asthma, bronchitis and allergies); improves some skin disorders, piles, boils; antifungal agent; used for insomnia; boosts immunity; helps protect against autoimmune diseases, particularly in combination with garlic

Fennel

Nutrients and minerals:	vitamins C and K, folate, amino acid arginine, flavinoids, high in iron, vitamin C, manganese
Scientific interest:	considerable

Reputed benefits:	good for anaemia (high iron levels and histidine stimulate haemoglobin production); aids digestion (which is why fennel seeds are often provided at the end of a meal); cures flatulence and constipation; disinfectant and antibacterial action (hence good for bacterial diarrhoea); respiratory disorders; stimulates milk secretion in nursing mothers; good antioxidant; anti-inflammatory; enhances immune system; gives protection against some cancers

Fenugreek

Nutrients and minerals:	dietary fibre, phytoestrogen, selenium, iron
Scientific interest:	moderate
Reputed benefits:	antioxidant and anti-inflammatory; assists with colds, sore throats; appears to act against cancer of the colon, prostrate and others; reduces fasting blood glucose levels and improves glucose tolerance in both Types 1 and 2 diabetes; aids digestion; weight control/loss (binds with dietary fats, reducing their absorption); heart conditions (possibly reduces LDL and VLDL cholesterol and triglycerides significantly without affecting HDL); assists in menopausal complaints; helps prevent hair loss

Garlic

One of the wonder foods of nature (although it has been suggested that those susceptible to migraines should treat it with caution).

Nutrients and minerals:	vitamins B1, B6, C, manganese, selenium, calcium, copper, zinc
Scientific interest:	extensive

Reputed benefits: heart disease (recognised ability to lower LDL cholesterol); improves circulation; reduces blood pressure; lowers triglyceride levels; boosts the immune system; boosts insulin production; antibiotic; antioxidant; anticoagulant; decongestant; natural antiseptic; has anticancer properties (can slow tumour growth, particularly of the breast, skin, colon and stomach); juice is antifungal

Ginger

Another of the wonder foods.

Nutrients and minerals: gingerols, various amino acids and other phytochemicals, vitamin B6, potassium, copper, manganese, calcium, selenium

Scientific interest: extensive

Reputed benefits: antioxidant; anti-inflammatory; motion sickness (particularly sea sickness); arthritis pain relief; safe and effective relief of nausea and vomiting during pregnancy; effective against intestinal gas; subject of ovarian cancer studies, and may inhibit growth of colorectal cancer cells

Mustard (seed or powder)

Nutrients and minerals: rich in tryptophan, Omega-3 fatty acids, vitamin B3 (niacin), contains phosphorus, manganese, iron, zinc, calcium, selenium

Scientific interest: extensive

Reputed benefits: anti-inflammatory and hence reduces severity of migraine and asthma; can provide protection against

heart attacks; may inhibit cancer cell growth in
gastrointestinal tract and colon

Nutmeg

The lone one with apparently not much going for it. Further, a negative has been reported – excessive amounts can cause problems, and it is very high in saturated fat.

Nutrients and minerals:	dietary fibre, manganese
Scientific interest:	moderate
Reputed benefits:	digestive problems – assists in overcoming nausea, vomiting, diarrhoea and gastroenteritis; possibly useful against insomnia, but frequent use should be avoided; for those trying to gain weight it increases appetite; antispasmodic

Pepper

Nutrients and minerals:	vitamin K, dietary fibre, manganese, iron
Scientific interest:	extensive
Reputed benefits:	powerful anti-oxidant; detoxifier; increases the absorption of other nutrients; anti-ageing; diuretic; antibacterial; improves digestion; stimulates breakdown of fat cells

Turmeric

Ginger and garlic have a well-earned food health reputation. Turmeric is not as well known, but it appears to be showing promise as the new super food.

Nutrients and minerals:	circumin, vitamins B6, C and K, iron (very high), manganese, potassium
Scientific interest:	moderate
Reputed benefits:	a potent anti-inflammatory, hence good against arthritis; powerful antioxidant; antiseptic; antibacterial;

used against jaundice, haemorrhage, flatulence, bruising, toothache, chest pain and colic; anti-cancer agent – studies have been conducted to investigate its efficacy against a range of cancers including cancer of the breast, pancreas, prostate, melanomas and leukaemia; detoxifies the liver; pain killer; skin benefits, including psoriasis; studies have shown promise with multiple sclerosis in mice, bowel disease, ulcerative colitis; may aid in the metabolism of fat and hence act as a weight control agent

An afterword

You will have noticed that many of the listed spices are reputed to improve the body's circulation – as a result of dilation of the blood vessels – and increase metabolism. Well, there can't be much doubt about the latter. If you need some tissues to mop the brow after eating a good curry, it's a sure sign that your metabolism has moved up a notch or two.

It should be noted that not all the benefits listed for the spices can be obtained through ingestion. Some are gained, or best gained, by external application in the form of a cream. The pain relieving effect of capsaicin for arthritis sufferers is one example of this.

A cautionary note

Please remember that this is a cookery book for curry fans, containing specialist knowledge of that field. It in no way pretends to be an authority on the medicinal properties of spices. We just wish to make the point that curries are a healthy food. Those with specific health problems, or considering taking concentrated doses of particular spices on a regular basis, should consult their health specialist, as some compounds contained within the spices are drugs and could interact with prescribed medication. In any case, it should be remembered that although some is good, a lot is not necessarily better and can, in fact, be dangerous. Nutmeg is an example of this.

Finally, the authors are at pains to remind you once again of the need for caution. Some studies point in one direction while a later one points in another. Nutrition is a complex field and foods can be double-edged swords. For instance, dietary fibre is without question 'good for us' and helps protect against intestinal tract cancers, but excessive fibre can bind with nutrients and so reduce their absorption.

However, notwithstanding the various uncertainties, over and over again studies have shown that the key to healthy eating is consuming fresh and natural foods, coupled with moderation and variety. On these generally accepted criteria, curries score well, with the value of the spices being beyond doubt.

Recipe page blanks

Home cooks tend to have a number of cookery books with an even greater number of handwritten recipes, written on scraps of paper and just stuffed between the pages. The organised few amongst us manage to get around to filing these in some orderly manner, but most of us don't. The result of this is that, as well as being untidy, it's usually hard to find the one you want when you want it.

To prevent this from happening yet again with this book, a few blank pages follow for you to record some of those additional curry recipes that you are sure to collect in the days ahead.

And finally...

If, during your cooking experimentation, you end up creating a masterpiece of your own, certainly share it with your friends. As a result, Peter's chicken vindaloo, Penelope's lamb madras and Paul's tarka dhal may well become locally famous. But you could aim higher and send it to the forum of www.undercovercurry.com and share it with the many. It could even go further. It is likely that at some future time the readers' recipes judged to be among the best will be included in a follow-up book in which you, as the recipe's creator, would naturally be acknowledged.

Recipe for: ....

From: ....

Recipe for: ....

From: ....

Recipe for: ....

From: ....

Recipe for: ....

From: ....

ADDENDUM

Being a curry purist, Dave was strongly of the opinion that the following recipe shouldn't be included in this book at all. However, he eventually agreed and it appeared in the 'Chicken Recipes' section. Then, just as the book was about to be printed, he recanted! Hmm...
What follows is what he wanted taken out.

Chicken tikka masala

As I've said, I don't really count this as a curry, so there was some doubt about including it. However, I accept that it's the most frequently ordered dish in the land and as it's a favourite, well... Got to keep everyone happy.

Now, there are almost as many different ways of making this dish as there are restaurants - certainly every restaurant I've ever worked in had their own version.

But to my mind the recipe which follows is one of the nicest of them all (although its sauce bears no resemblance whatsoever to that mythical original one). It is, though, so different and unusual that I expect it will surprise you. However, be assured that if you cook this one for your loved ones, it (and therefore you) will get the big seal of approval.

(By the way, the myth about the origins of the sauce goes like this. A customer was not satisfied with the dryness of his chicken tikka so he complained to the waiter about it. The waiter took the dish back to the kitchen and passed on the complaint to the chef, who responded by swiftly adding a can of tomato soup mixed with spices and some cream, and wondrously, a marvellous new sauce was created. This supposedly happened in a restaurant in Glasgow, but unfortunately it's just a myth – as the guy who created the myth has admitted.)

....

- tin of fruit cocktail (!)
- pkt. of either ground almonds *or* ground cashew nuts (or half of each is also nice)
- sultanas (handful)
- cream
- sugar (2 dessertspoons)
- tandoori marinade
- prepared chicken tikka (see page 42)
- (food colouring)

  For the optional addition
  - ghee
  - garlic (2 handfuls, chopped)
  - Kashuri methi leaf, dried

....

1. The sauce is done in the blender; all the ingredients go straight into it.
2. Open your can of **fruit cocktail** (no, this is not a misprint), but half of it will be enough.
3. Add the **ground nuts** you've selected.
4. Toss in a handful of **sultanas**.
5. Add enough **cream** to about ¾ fill your blender. (They usually use UHT single cream in the restaurants.)
6. Add the **sugar** (2 dessertspoons)…
7. …and about two curry spoons of **tandoori marinade.** (If there's not enough redness to give the mixture a light pink colour, add a little red food colouring.)
8. Now really blitz the blender's contents until it's *completely* smooth. It must not be even slightly gritty.

9. Place the **chicken tikka** into a pan and pour in enough of the blender's mixture to completely cover it, stir, and turn the heat up to high. Keep stirring. As the mixture reduces, its colour becomes stronger, turning from a light pink to a pinkish red – and there's the creamy sauce done.

The optional addition

This is an additional, three step beginning to the recipe.

    (i) Start with a pan, say, ⅓ full of **ghee,** melted.

    (ii) Throw in two handfuls of **chopped garlic** and a good handful of **methi leaf.**

    (iii) Fry them together until the garlic starts to go brown. Transfer the pan's contents to the blender.

Now proceed with the steps previously given – the ½ tin of fruit cocktail…

....

Either version makes an absolutely wonderful dish, even if I say so myself. (But I still think they shouldn't be in the book.)

So might Dave Loyden be a little upset when he sees this inclusion? Could be.
Oh, well.
(Hang onto this copy of the book. I don't think the recipe will be included in the first reprint – or in any other, for that matter!)

Happy cooking.